Charles Isaac Elton

Account of Shelley's Visits to France, Switzerland, and Savoy

In the Years 1814 and 1816

Charles Isaac Elton

Account of Shelley's Visits to France, Switzerland, and Savoy
In the Years 1814 and 1816

ISBN/EAN: 9783337155186

Printed in Europe, USA, Canada, Australia, Japan

Cover: Foto ©Andreas Hilbeck / pixelio.de

More available books at **www.hansebooks.com**

AN ACCOUNT OF SHELLEY'S VISITS TO FRANCE SWITZERLAND AND SAVOY IN THE YEARS 1814 AND 1816

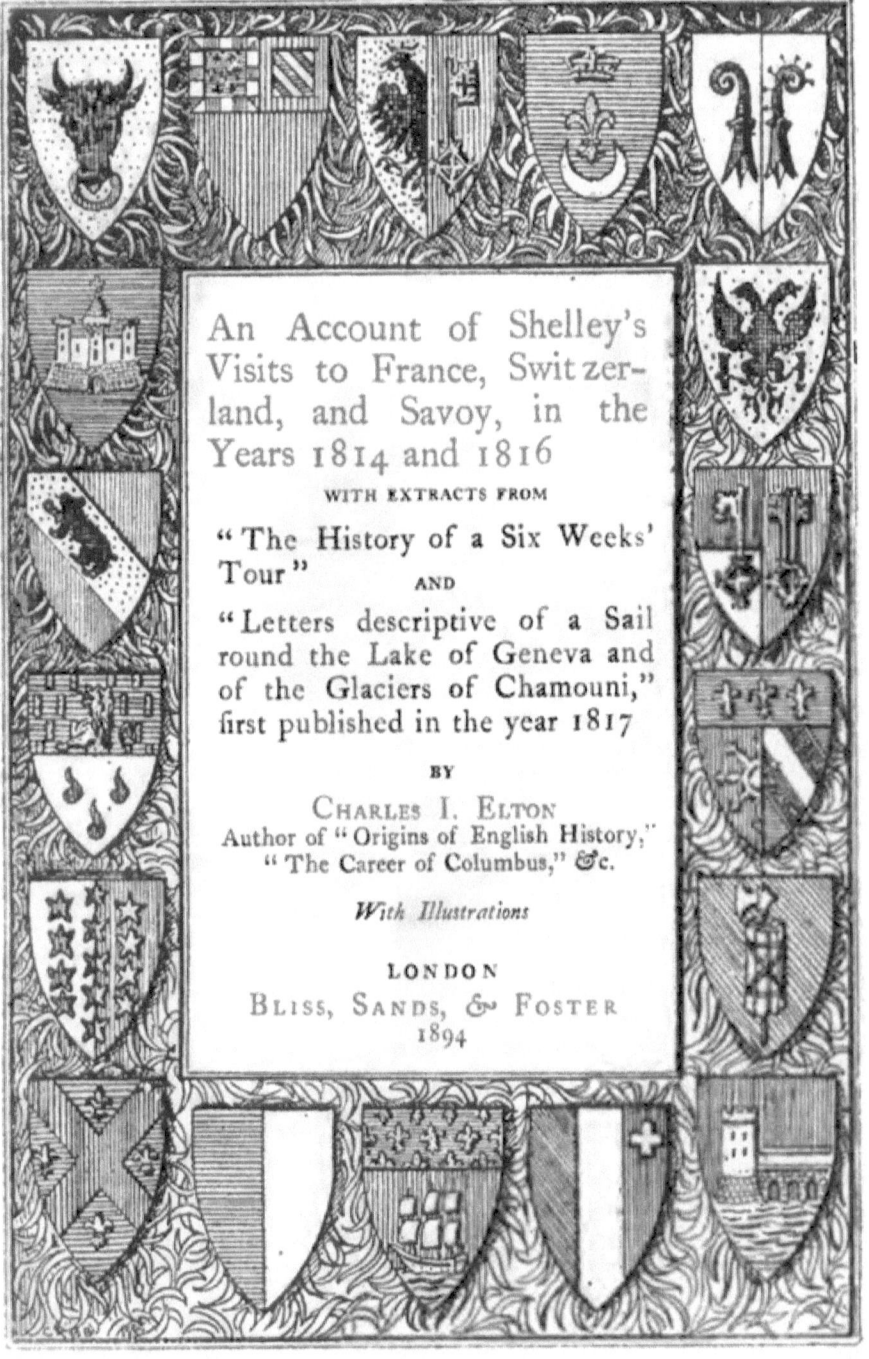

An Account of Shelley's Visits to France, Switzerland, and Savoy, in the Years 1814 and 1816

WITH EXTRACTS FROM

"The History of a Six Weeks' Tour"   AND

"Letters descriptive of a Sail round the Lake of Geneva and of the Glaciers of Chamouni," first published in the year 1817

BY

CHARLES I. ELTON
Author of "Origins of English History," "The Career of Columbus," &c.

With Illustrations

LONDON
BLISS, SANDS, & FOSTER
1894

TABLE OF CONTENTS

		Page
1.	Introduction	1
2.	Tour of 1814: France	15
3.	Tour of 1814: Switzerland and the Rhine	33
4.	Tour of 1816: The Lake of Geneva	45
5.	Tour of 1816: Chamouni	68
6.	A list of the principal works to which reference has been made	105
7.	Extracts:	
	I. History of a Six Weeks' Tour—Preface	111
	II. Introduction	113
	III. France	114
	IV. Switzerland and the Rhine	131
	V. Germany	141
	VI. Holland	147

Page

8. Letters written during a residence of three months in the Environs of Geneva in the Summer of 1816 :

    Letter I. 151

    Letter II. 157

    Letter III. 161

    Letter IV. 173

9. Mont Blanc. Lines written in the Vale of Chamouni 190

    Index 197

LIST OF ILLUSTRATIONS

Photogravure

Portrait of Shelley . . . *Frontispiece*

Etchings

Swiss Châlets . . . . *To face page* 34
Porte St.-Denis 118

Pen-and-ink Sketches

Pilatus . . . . . *To face page* 10
Besançon 28
Stolzenfels 40
Rotterdam 44
Chillon 64
Mont Blanc: Lac de Chède . . . 78
Mer de Glace 96
Neuchâtel 132
Rheinstein 142

Cologne . . . . . *To face page*	146
Lausanne	170
Cluse	176
Glacier des Bossons	184

SHELLEY'S VISITS TO FRANCE, SWITZERLAND, AND SAVOY

INTRODUCTION

THE object of this essay is to illustrate the little volume containing the history of Shelley's six weeks' tour, and the letters on Chamouni and the environs of Geneva, which first appeared in 1817 without any author's name, but were eventually recognised as being "Shelley's publication." Nothing, said Mrs. Shelley, who took herself a great share in the work, could possibly be more unpresuming than the account of their desultory visits to places which are now familiar to us all. It has ceased to be interesting in itself to hear of a journey up the Rhine, or to the English colony at Montreux, or to receive the last description of the beauties of Geneva or Lucerne. But, after all, the "castled Rhine" will never lose the charm thrown over it by the writer of "Childe Harold," nor Meillerie and Mont Blanc cease to be transfigured by Shelley's romantic visions. We do not care so much for what they actually saw as for the picture of their eager pursuit of an "inconstant summer of delight." In order to understand that state of mind it is necessary to examine the poems composed in connection with these journeys, including, besides the "Lines to Mont Blanc" and the "Hymn to Intellectual Beauty," several later poems, and a few more fragments that appear to contain allusions to the original journals and letters. Apart from mere reminiscences of scenery, the thought underlying most of these poems is the idea that the beauty of Nature is the friend and companion of Man: the phenomena of the universe are regarded as existing in the observer's mind, while that mind and all that belongs to it may be viewed apart as one of the forms presented in Nature. We shall find that both Shelley and Byron continually return to this idea; and it seems clear that in their dealings with the subject they both owed something to Wordsworth.

We may be sure that Shelley cared little for the "Excursion"; but it is easy to see that he was influenced by certain portions of its preface. Wordsworth had intended to construct a vast work, for which the "Excursion" was to serve as an introduction, the two being related to each other "as the antechapel to the body of a Gothic church." The minor pieces, which had long been before the world, were to be referred to the same design, and might be likened to "the little cells, and oratories, and sepulchral recesses." "The Recluse," as the whole work was to be called, never advanced very far towards completion; but its author placed in the preface to "The Excursion" a passage from its first book to serve as a clue to his argument. The description of Beauty, in the form of Imagination, follows his invocation of Milton's "heavenly muse" and Shakespeare's "prophetic spirit" for help in his exploration of the human mind, in which he found the haunt and the main region of his song:

> Beauty, a living presence of the earth,
> Surpassing the most fair ideal forms
> Which craft and delicate spirits have composed
> From earth's materials, waits upon my steps,
> Pitches her tents before me as I move,
> An hourly neighbour.

In Wordsworth's theory we may either say that man's intellect is framed to receive all Nature, or that the Universe itself is "fitted to the mind." The point is recognised both by Shelley and Byron in their pictures of the country round Montreux. In the one case we may refer to the poem on "Intellectual Beauty," and in the other to the Third Canto of "Childe Harold," and its writer's own notes upon the poem. Byron, one would suppose, gained some of his insight from conversations with Shelley, although the younger man acknowledged the complete supremacy of one whose conceptions rose fast and fair "as perfect worlds at the Creator's will." Shelley certainly outstripped Wordsworth in finding the delicate meanings that underlie the forms of Nature. "What is your substance, whereof are you made, that millions of strange shadows on you tend?" There had been a mightier spirit before them, skilled far beyond their powers in "dreaming of things to come," and in all these thoughts they were in fact depending on what Shakespeare had given to the world :

> Hither as to their fountain other stars,
> Repairing, in their golden urns draw light.

Let us take Byron's picture of Clarens and the opposite heights. He is dealing with Rousseau, his "self-torturing sophist," who in 1759 had associated his "Nouvelle Héloise" with the broad lake and the Alps frowning in bastions and parallels :

> 'Tis lone,
> And wonderful and deep, and hath a sound,
> And sense, and sight of sweetness : here the Rhone
> Hath spread himself a couch, the Alps have reared a throne.

In describing the voyage round the lake he acknowledged that it would be difficult to deny the peculiar adaptation of the whole region to the events associated with their scenery in literature. "But this is not all," says Byron; "if the great writer had not chosen these scenes as the setting of his work, the same kind of associations would have belonged to them; and perhaps they have done for him what no human being could do for them." The feeling, he adds, with which Clarens and the rocks of Meillerie are invested, is of a higher and more comprehensive order than any mere sympathy with individual passion. "It is the great principle of the universe, which is there condensed, but not less manifested; of which knowing ourselves to be a part, we lose our individuality and mingle in the beauty of the whole." The same thoughts appear in those portions of "Childe Harold" which were written under the influence of the same scenery. "I live not in myself, but I become portion of that around me:" and again he cries:

> Are not the mountains, waves, and skies, a part
> Of me and of my soul, as I of them?
> Is not the love of these deep in my heart
> With a pure passion?

At Clarens, his "sweet Clarens," Byron found every aspect of Nature charged with the "breath of passionate thought"; it is the home of Love, "who here ascends a throne, to which the steps are mountains." As one looks across the lake at sunrise or sunset, the peaks above Meillerie flame pink or red-hot as an oven, according to the structure of the mountain, and the ice-fields of Mont Blanc shine like the pure angel-gold; and Shelley adds the colours of fire and amethyst seen in masses of cloud that roll on the mountain-side "while the sunset sleeps upon its snow." To Byron everything around told of a world of beauty and love: "The snows above, the very glaciers have his colours caught, and sunset into rose-hues sees them wrought." The flower knows his presence, and the air his "soft and summer breath":

> All things are here of him: from the black pines
> Which are his shade on high, and the loud roar
> Of torrents where he listeneth, to the vines
> Which slope his green path downward to the shore,
> When the bowed waters meet him and adore,
> Kissing his feet with murmurs.

Shelley's "Hymn to Intellectual Beauty" was an out-come of the same expedition. We may detect in it some echo of the lines from "The Recluse," and some tone of Milton's "Uranian lute": its inner meaning is to be found in that phrase, already noticed, where youth is shown "pursuing, like the swallow, the inconstant summer of delight and beauty that invests this visible world." It was upon the mutability of the presence, the fleeting shadow of an unseen Power, that his mind was most inclined to reflect : it passes, he thought, with an inconstant wing " as summer winds that creep from flower to flower " :

> Spirit of Beauty, that dost consecrate
> With thine own hues all thou dost shine upon
> Of human thought or form, where art thou gone?
> Why dost thou pass away, and leave our state,
> This dim vast vale of tears, vacant and desolate?
> Ask why the sunlight not for ever
> Weaves rainbows o'er yon mountain-river,
> Why aught should fail and fade that once is shown.

His emotional temperament was excited by reading a fine description of the Lake in the place where the picture had been drawn. He uses the words of passionate affection in dilating on the prospect before his eyes. At Clarens he found it hard to repress " the tears of melancholy transport "; and in addressing the influence that brought the beauty of Nature into his mind, he broke into a similar rapture :

> I vowed that I would dedicate my powers
> To thee and thine : have I not kept the vow?
> With beating heart and streaming eyes, even now
> I call the phantoms of a thousand hours,
> Each from his voiceless grave.

The poem on Mont Blanc represents the

same kind of feeling, with some variation of form. The Universe flows through the mind, "and rolls its rapid waves": and the soul in "unremitting interchange" receives ideas from without, and renders life to the phænomena of Nature. Shelley gave his own account of the poem at the end of the preface to the "Six Weeks' Tour": "It was composed under the immediate impression of the deep and powerful feelings excited by the objects which it attempts to describe; and, as an undisciplined overflowing of the soul, rests its claim to approbation on an attempt to imitate the untameable wildness and inaccessible solemnity from which those feelings sprang." The poem on "Spiritual Beauty" had dealt with frailty and mutability: the "Ode to Mont Blanc" teaches the permanence of those forces by which are sustained "the earth and stars and sea":

> The secret strength of things
> Which governs thought, and to the infinite dome
> Of heaven is as a law, inhabits thee.

Shelley had left his cottage at Montalègre on the 20th of July 1816, and arrived at the entrance to the Valley of Servoz on the afternoon of the following day. "Mont Blanc was before us!" he writes: "Mont Blanc was before us, but it was covered with cloud: its base, furrowed with dreadful gaps, was seen above. Pinnacles of snow intolerably bright, part of the chain connected with Mont Blanc, shone through the clouds at intervals on high. I never knew, I never imagined, what mountains were before? There was a wooden bridge, called the Pont Pélissier, which spanned the Arve and its ravine: here Shelley stood before the vision of the dazzling mountains that 'glittered though a chasm of the clouds'; and here the poem was inspired, as he lingered on the bridge. On that evening they passed close to the Glacier des Bossons, which overhung the woods and meadows with an icy precipice, 'winding through its own ravine like a bright belt flung over the region of pines.' The next day was given to rest; but on the 23rd Shelley went with his companions to the source of the Arveiron, and saw the ice-cave and the jagged rim of the Glacier des Bois: 'we saw, as we sat on a rock, masses of ice detach themselves from on high, and rush with a loud dull noise into the vale.' In the evening, Shelley visited the Glacier des Bossons, and was deeply impressed by the shattered trees and desert of stones at its base, and the pinnacles above, "like spires of radiant crystal, covered with a network of frosted silver." The poem as it stands was finished that same night; but in Mr. Rossetti's edition there are a few fragmentary lines showing that Shelley had intended to add an allusion to the noise of the breaking glacier:

> It is the roar
> Of the rent ice-cliffs, which the sunbeams call,
> Plunging into the vale: it is the blast
> Descending on the pines.

In the earlier portion of the same poem there is a reference to one of the waterfalls in the valley of the Arve. We are shown the crags clothed with pines, and the river foaming in rifts cut like caverns through the rock:

> When power in likeness of the Arve comes down
> From the ice-gulfs that gird his secret throne,
> Bursting through these dark mountains like the flame
> Of lightning through the tempest.

Within a short space the travellers saw two streams shot from a great height into the valley. "The first fell from the overhanging brow of a bleak precipice on an enormous rock, precisely resembling some colossal Egyptian statue of a female deity." The water struck the head of the image, and fell on both sides in cloudy foam, "imitating a veil of the most exquisite woof." Uniting itself again, the stream concealed the lower portion of the statue, and hid in a winding of its channel, where it burst into a deeper fall. We quote a passage from the invocation addressed by the poet to the "many-coloured, many-voicèd vale":

> Thine earthly rainbows stretched across the sleep
>   Of the ethereal waterfall, whose veil
> Robes some unsculptured image: the strange sleep
>   Which when the voices of the desert fail
> Wraps all in its own deep eternity;
> Thy caverns echoing to the Arve's commotion,
>   A loud lone sound no other sound may tame,
> Thou art pervaded by that ceaseless motion,
>   Thou art the path of that unresting sound.

A few allusions to Shelley's Swiss tours may be found in his later poems. The Vale of Chamouni, for instance, might have supplied the type of the hanging snow-fields and ice-girt pinnacles in the "Sonnet to the Nile." The allegory of the "Two Spirits" contains stanzas that remind us of a legend from Lucerne. One may read it in the first of the delightful letters of Victor Hugo to his Adèle, where he describes the marvels of Pilatus: there was a colossal pine, they told him, which stood alone on the cliff, and on each of its spreading limbs grew another pine, so that it looked like a seven-branched candlestick. Shelley may have heard the story at Lucerne or Brunnen, though neither Pilatus nor any of its companions is named in the journal:

> Some say there is a precipice
>   Where one vast pine is frozen to ruin,
> O'er piles of snow and chasms of ice,
>   'Mid Alpine mountains;

> And that the languid storm pursuing
>   That wingèd shape for ever flies
> Round those hoar branches, aye renewing
>   Its aëry fountains.

Shelley did not see the cliffs in their winter desolation: but he had read and talked about the pendant icicles, the snow-wreaths, and the torrent frozen into a blue-veined mass, like the treasure in the caves of crystal. The scene appears in a poem composed only a few months after his wanderings round the lake. "It was at the season," he writes, "when the Earth up-springs from slumber":

> 'Twas at this season that Prince Athanase
>   Passed the white Alps. Those eagle-baffling mountains
> Slept in their shrouds of snow. Beside the ways
>   The waterfalls were voiceless; for their fountains
> Were changed to mines of sunless crystal now,
>   Or by the curdling winds, like brazen wings
> Which clanged along the mountain's marble brow,
>   Warped into adamantine fretwork hung
> And filled with frozen light the chasm below.

Though the "Prometheus Unbound" was not finished till the later visit to Rome, it is clear that it contains many passages based either on the Six Weeks' Tour or the visit to Chamouni. Some of these will be discussed later; but we may just mention the "crawling glaciers," the springs stagnating "with white wrinkled frost," and the roseate sunlight quivering through "peaks of cloud-like snow." The last phrase recalls that fine passage in the Journal where the travellers describe their first sight of the Alps. "They were a hundred miles distant, but they reach so high in the heavens that they looked like those accumulated clouds of dazzling white that arrange themselves on the horizon during summer." And in a letter from Sécheron we are shown the Alps glowing in that rose-like hue "which attends the clouds of an autumnal sky when the daylight is almost gone." In another part of the poem we find an evident reference to the drive from Les Rousses to the Lake of Geneva. There was a complaint that the plains of snow were only broken by scattered pine-trees and poles set up to mark the road. "No river or rock-encircled lawn relieved the eye;" and when the tortured Prometheus is speaking of the beauty of life, he calls up a very similar scene:

> Of rock-embosomed lawns and snow-fed streams,
> Now seen athwart from vapours deep below.

We shall learn from the journals of their first expedition how Shelley rejoiced in the scenery of the Rhine. He saw the river in its glorious vintage-season and compared it to "the loveliest paradise on earth"; and we perceive that he is thinking of the Rhine when the voice of 'Asia' is heard singing of the magical boat on the river that rolls towards the sea:

> It seems to float, ever, for ever,
> Upon that many-winding river,
> Between mountains, woods, abysses,
> A paradise of wildernesses.

Whoever has seen the Castle of Chillon will recollect the little Ile de Paix, which Byron rightly picked out as causing a very peculiar effect upon the view, from its solitude and diminutive size: "A small green isle, it seemed no more, scarce broader than my dungeon-floor." We cannot tell whether Shelley wrote on this subject at the time of his visit; but on looking at the later fragments there is a picture of an islet, with young flowers and shady trees, which cannot be mistaken, more especially as we are told that it was girdled by the waves, " with which the clouds and mountains pave a lake's blue chasm ":

> There was a little lawny islet,
> By anemone and violet,
>   Like mosaic, paven:
> And its roof was flowers and leaves,
> Which the summer's breath inweaves,
> Where nor sun, nor showers nor breeze,
> Pierce the pines and tallest trees,
>   Like a gem engraven.

TOUR OF 1814: FRANCE

WE now proceed to take the little Journal in hand, in order to follow the young travellers in the course of their simple adventures. Our business is concerned with what they saw, and more especially with the effect of the scenery upon Shelley's imagination. We have nothing to do here with their family troubles or private affairs, except that we may perhaps notice some of their odd shifts when in pawn at Paris, or scraping their way home by the cheapest conveyance, after magnificent dreams of a winter in Italy. This first tour took place in 1814, very soon after the deposition of Napoleon; but the printed account did not appear till 1817, some months after their second expedition to Switzerland. In making the full extracts that form a great portion of our work, it has been thought convenient to modernise the spelling, except in the case of a few local names, of which the old-fashioned forms still remain in partial use. We shall keep to the initials of the original, instead of inserting the travellers' own names in the modern way. It will be observed that M. stands for "Mary," and C. for "Claire," as Miss Clairmont generally called herself. It may be also noticed that M. and C. are described as sisters, although they were not really related, the one being Godwin's daughter by his marriage with Mary Wollstonecraft, and the other the daughter of his second wife by her former marriage. The various omissions of passages and phrases occurring in the Journal and Letters relate for the most part to indiscriminate attacks upon large classes of people, which it is only fair to ascribe to some passing influence of the heat or bad weather. The omissions from the Swiss Letters relate partly to similar cases, and partly to misquotations from Horace and Tacitus, made at a distance from books and left uncorrected by accident, as well as to the various attempts at identifying places mentioned by Rousseau, when by his own published statement such efforts could never succeed.

"It is now nearly three years since the journey took place," says Mrs. Shelley in her Introduction to the work; "and the diary then kept was not very copious." She had arranged its contents as well as she could, with the addition of several letters from Switzerland; and she could only regret that the materials were not more complete. The party reached Dover on Thursday, July 28, 1814. They had reasons for wishing to cross without delay, and declined to wait for the morning packet, which might contain visitors whom they did not wish to meet. They watched her next day from Calais, beating her wings for hours in vain attempts to reach the harbour.

Shelley had hired a smack on the evening of their arrival, hoping to sail pleasantly across to France in two or three hours. The weather of 1814 was hotter than had been known for many years. The little vessel crept out, but was nearly becalmed, and the sail "flapped in the flagging breeze"; but later on a fresh wind sprang up, and the moonbeams glanced on the marching waves, "like the path of some sweet water-sprite, on the heaving and desolate sea." A rack of clouds piled itself above a red and stormy horizon: "the fast-flashing lightning became pale in the breaking day." We seem to be present, and to share their alarms: a "thunder-squall" strikes the sail: but the wind veers and drives the smack before it, and at last the sun rises with a broad red face above the pier.

They are delighted with the old hotel and the look of the people in the streets. They saw ladies with hair trained into stiff towers, decked in ribbons or flowers a yard above their eyebrows, and market-women in great starched caps; and they liked the boatmen in earrings, and the fishwives whom Wordsworth scolded for being so withered and grotesque, "and shrill and fierce in accent." Like other tourists, they were cheered by the thought that the English had been masters of Calais and the Pale for two centuries before Queen Mary died. Two of the party went outside the ramparts to inspect the defences, which seemed to the ladies to consist of "fields where the hay was making." A graver traveller had written a technical account, when the escarpments were not fifty years old: "the town," says Mr. Ray, "is very strongly fortified after the modern fashion, with an impenetrable wall and bastions of earth, and a deep trench of water to the landward."

On Saturday afternoon they started for Boulogne in a cabriolet with three horses, the harness as usual being composed of ropes and thongs: the queer pig-tailed postillion cracked his whip as they clattered over the Chaussée, and "an old forlorn shepherd with a cocked hat" gazed sadly after their equipage. At Paris it was too hot for sight-seeing: they walked in the trim gardens of the Tuileries, but preferred the delightful Boulevards, the Porte St. Denis in its splendour, and the fountain, or say rather "the superb cascade," which used to spout perfume on a Coronation-day. After talking over many plans, they fixed upon one which was both pleasant and eccentric. "We resolved to walk through France": "and we determined to purchase an ass, to carry our portmanteau and one of us by turns." No sooner said than done; and on Monday, the 8th of August, Shelley and Miss Clairmont "went to the ass-market and purchased an ass." The regular course would have been to go next day to the horse-market at the Barrière de St. Victor. Captain Medwin tells us that they found what was wanted at the Marché des Herbes, where it seems that they bought a costermonger's donkey, which broke down at once under the portmanteau. We remember, when Don Quixote left his village, how Sancho Panza rode like a patriarch with wallet and bottle, and his master stood pensive awhile, wondering if any one had ever heard of a knight with a squire "so assishly mounted." He could not discover any authority; but thought that his squire might use the beast for a time, resolving to accommodate him more honourably upon the next occasion. The first evening of the tour was spent at Charenton, in the winding valley of the Seine. "Oh! this is beautiful enough; let us live here," cried the youngest of the trio. "We were merry enough," says the Diarist, "and thought the leagues short;"

but in fact they were plodding slowly enough, and were hardly three miles from Paris when they came to their journey's end. Finding the ass useless, the writer continued, they sold it as soon as they arrived, and bought a mule for ten napoleons. They started next morning, "clad in black silk," and soon reached the shady woodlands, and lunched, not like the knight-errant on Spanish ham and acorns, but on a long loaf and good fruit; and they drank their *eau rougie*, thinking of Don Quixote and **Sancho**.

They slept that night at Guignes, a village set in the midst of a wide plain between the streams of the Yvron and Ancœur. **The place had been** the scene of great events in the earlier part of the **year,** when Napoleon had rallied his forces there, and had rolled back the Austrians and Bavarians on the road to Troyes. Four of his Marshals were posted **with** their divisions in the immediate neighbourhood. His own headquarters were at Guignes on February the 16th, **the** day before the battle of Mormant; and he took the opportunity of reviewing the division of Dragoons which General Trelliard had just brought from Bayonne, and about a thousand of the Grenadiers and Chasseurs, who had arrived from the army of the Pyrenees or had been collected in the *dépôts* of the Guard. The Comte de Valmy had brought in his cavalry the evening before. "We slept at Guignes," says the Diary, "in the same room and beds in which Napoleon and some of his Generals had rested during the late war: the little old woman of the place was highly gratified in having this little story to tell."

At Provins they left the dreary plain, and were delighted with the "Tour de César" and the crumbling battlements of the Upper Town, "and the ancient church of St. Quiriace, to which the ruined castle serves as a belfry. The irregular scene looked like a bit for a painter, and was " a delicious relief to the eye." They had "nearly forgotten" the war; but they soon found themselves on the track of the Cossacks. Nogent, we are told, had been entirely desolated by these barbarians, who perhaps remembered Moscow and the plunder of the Russian villages. All the miseries of the war were doubtless attributed to the savage warriors under the Hetman Platow; but as a matter of fact there were very few Russians present when Nogent was destroyed. Being a small open town, it was doubtful whether the place should be defended; but General Bourmont finding the new works useless, and indeed hardly begun, determined to resist the Austrians in the ancient fashion. The streets were barricaded, the houses loopholed, and a villa called the Belvedere was converted into a fortified post. The Count de Pahlen delivered his attack on the 11th of February, and after a desperate struggle of forty hours found that he had lost 1800 men, and had only taken a few outlying houses. The town was shelled and set on fire at several points; but the defence was kept up manfully until orders were received for a retreat upon Provins. General Bourmont was wounded; but Colonel Voirol, who had taken the command, carried off his force after blowing up the bridge, together with a Russian officer and fifty Cossacks advancing too eagerly in pursuit. A little beyond Nogent the travellers left the *Grande Route*, and struck across the plains towards Troyes. They arrived at St. Aubin about sunset, and thought it "a lovely village," as it stood embowered in foliage; but on a nearer view the cottages were found to be roofless and the rafters black. There were a few inhabitants remaining, and the visitors asked for milk, as they had far to go before night: "They had none to give: all their cows had been taken by the Cossacks." Village after village, as they advanced through the chalky plain, presented nothing to the sight but broken walls, charred beams, and gardens white with dust and plaster. Some of the descriptions are so repelling in their details that we omit to produce them again. It may be taken for granted that a place lately ransacked or taken by storm will offer little in itself or in the looks of its ruined inhabitants, that will please the visitor's taste. At Echemine only the inn remained standing, and the villagers were camping out in a sad state of misery. The English travellers were not very cordially received: "these people did not know that Napoleon had been deposed," though the treaty between the new King and the Allies had been signed on the 1st of June. Asked why they did not rebuild the cottages, the people said that they were afraid the Cossacks would destroy them on their return. Perhaps they knew more about Napoleon and the Cossacks than their foreign visitors supposed. But at Pavillon, where no such great ravages had occurred, " we might have fancied ourself," says the Diary, " in another quarter of the globe." All was cleanliness and hospitality; the people were building up the houses that had been destroyed. "What could occasion so great a difference?" Shelley refers to these events again in the preface to the "Revolt of Islam": "I have seen the theatre of the more visible ravages of tyranny and war; cities and villages reduced to scattered groups of black and roofless houses, and the naked inhabitants sitting famished on their desolated households."

Such troubles befell the party at Troyes that there was no time to write about the town, except to note that it seemed dirty and uninviting, and that some of the suburbs were destroyed. Shelley had hurt his ankle and was totally incapable of walking, and the rest of them were in nearly as bad a condition. The mule and its saddle were given away for a mere song; and they determined to buy a little open carriage, and to engage a *voiturier* with another mule to take them on to Neuchâtel. The first of a series of quarrels with the *voiturier* began on leaving the town. It arose, according to the Journal, out of "a curious instance of French vanity"; but it turned out that the coachman was right in the main. He pointed to the flat country between the Seine and Barce, and said that there had been a battle on that ground between the French and the Russians. "The Russians got the victory," laughs the lady. "Ah, Madame! the French are never beaten," the driver replies; and he explains that the defeated Russians had only occupied the town by wheeling round "in a circuitous route." The French, in fact, had not been defeated at Troyes, though the town had several times changed hands. On the 1st of February Napoleon was badly beaten by Blücher at La Rothière, in the valley of the Aube; falling back on Troyes, after winning a battle at Rouay, he occupied the town on the 3rd and left it on the 6th, when it was immediately occupied by the Army of Silesia. Napoleon returned on February the 23rd, and found that Blücher had left only an Austrian brigade to hold the place. The Emperor commenced an attack, and was about to order an assault, when he received a message that the town would be evacuated during the night, but that if the cannonade were continued it would first be set on fire. Napoleon entered the town on the next morning, and it was held by the French till March the 4th. When the attack had begun, after the Austrian general had declined to surrender, the garrison had replied by a fire of shells and grenades which set the suburbs of St. Martin and Ste. Savine in flames. On the 4th of March, Marshal Macdonald again evacuated Troyes, which was at once occupied by the combined Austrian and Russian forces; and we are told that the Allies used their opportunity very unmercifully, and gave the town up for two days to every kind of licence. There was, indeed, no occasion on which it could properly be said that the Allies entered Troyes after winning a battle upon the adjoining plains.

The village of Vandœuvres had suffered considerably in the war; but the party found a castle close by, with grounds laid out in the English style, and they were allowed to ramble as they pleased, and to rest in the green shade of a wood. At the next turn of the road they entered the narrow valley of the Aube, and were delighted with the vine-wreathed hills rising steep out of the meadows streaked with lines of willows and poplars. The country churches still reared their glittering spires, which "the Cossacks" had forgotten to destroy. Some of the most romantic sites, however, were filled with the ruins of hamlets destroyed by fire ; but these for the most part had been burned by the French themselves when Oudinot was retreating from La Rothière.

Bar-sur-Aube is a small town standing at the foot of Mont St^e. Germaine, at that narrow opening into the valley " where the hills abruptly terminate." Our travellers made an ascent for a view, but were caught in mist and rain : "the laden clouds," said Shelley, "made the darkness almost as deep as at midnight, but in the west an unusually brilliant and fiery redness occupied an opening in the vapours." At the gates of Bar they bid the mountains "a short farewell": but they found that Chaumont was set on a steep elevation above the Marne, and that Langres occupied a **lofty plateau**. This town is now a very strong fortress ; but at the time of their visit there were only remains of old and scanty works of defence. From a point at the edge of this plateau it is possible to see Mont Blanc, about a hundred and eighty miles away. Looking towards the Jura about sunset, the head of the mountain shows like a star above the purple ridges on the horizon, just as the white marble of Milan Cathedral can be seen at sunrise as a glittering point of light from the summit of Monte Rosa. M. de la Condamine mentioned the fact as early as 1773 in the remarks on the mountains and ice-valleys of Switzerland embodied in his " Journal of a Tour to Italy." " Mont Cenis," he said, " is the highest mountain of the Alps: yet the White Mountain that we see from the banks of the Lake of Geneva, and the upper half of which is always covered with snow, is incomparably much higher." He adds that this White Mountain, not included by him among the Alps, must be four thousand feet higher than the Pike of Teneriffe, which is oddly described as having passed for "the highest mountain of Europe": " the White Mountain is also seen from the environs of Langres at sixty leagues distance, where they distinguish its summit covered with snow above the chain of Mount Jura." It is evident from what they said that the travellers had no suspicion of the fact. It was not, indeed, till they had entered Switzerland that they saw what they had so long desired. " Two leagues from Neuchâtel we saw the Alps : range after range of black mountains are seen extending one before the other, and far behind all, towering above every feature of the scene, the snowy Alps."

The description of the country round Besançon is very skilfully contrived. The hills appeared in the distance during the whole day as the party drew near to the town; but they were quite unprepared for the view that met their eyes in the morning. As they passed out of the gate they saw that the town stood as it were on a peninsula of rock, shut in by the River Doubs, "in a horse-shoe curve." The gateway itself had been cut out of the live rock by the Roman workmen who had built the aqueduct. The road wound under the wall of a precipice, and in front rose a rocky amphitheatre of hills thickly covered with vines. " This approach to mountain scenery filled us with delight," said the travellers; but it was otherwise with the *voiturier* who came from the plains of Troyes; for these hills, we are told, so utterly scared him, "that in some degree he lost his reason." The man appears to have been both sulky and perverse: but we need not attribute his dark moods to anything like lunacy. The idea may have been an after-thought, suggested by Shelley's feelings when he stood under the pinnacles of Mont Blanc, and felt his spirit breath-

less before "the harmony of Nature": "the immensity of those aërial summits, when they suddenly burst upon the sight, excited a sentiment of ecstatic wonder not unallied to madness." Goethe made a remark of much the same kind when Eckermann complained of the "uncomfortable feeling" produced by the gloomy sublimity of the Alps upon one who was born in the plains. "The feeling is natural," said Goethe: "Switzerland, at first, made so great an impression on me, that it disturbed and confused me; only after repeated visits, only in after-years, when I visited those mountains merely as a mineralogist, could I feel at my ease among them."

It seems that the mule broke down under the task of drawing four persons and their luggage in a four-wheeled carriage, though the tourists put down its master's disobliging mood to the fact that "the hills had scared his senses." At any rate, they were compelled to remain many hours at the hamlet of Mort almost as soon as they began to mount the hills again. The journey was resumed before sunrise. The road led to the west of the range that encircle the plateau of Besançon. From the top they saw the whole expanse of the valley filled with a white undulating mist, which was pierced by the piny mountains, like islands: "the sun had just risen, and a ray of red light lay upon the waves of this fluctuating vapour; to the west, opposite the sun, it seemed driven by the light against the rocks in immense masses of foaming cloud, until it became lost in the distance, mixing its tints with the fleecy sky."

The incident is closely reproduced in the dialogue between Asia and Panthea in the "Prometheus Unbound." Asia and her sister are seen on a pinnacle of rock among mountains, in the realm of Demogorgon. "How glorious art thou, Earth!" cries Asia, ready almost to fall and worship the beauties of creation:

> Even now my heart adoreth. Wonderful!
> Look, sister, ere the vapour dim thy brain:
> Beneath is a wide plain of billowy mist,
> As a lake, paving in the morning sky
> With azure waves which burst in silver light,
> Some Indian vale. Behold it, rolling on
> Under the curdling winds, and islanding
> The peak whereon we stand, midway, around,
> Encinctured by the dark and blooming forests,
> Dim twilight-lawns and stream-illumined caves,
> And wind-enchanted shapes of wandering mist.

The effects of the "ray of red light" upon the masses of foaming cloud, and the scattering of its tints "through a fleecy sky," are reproduced in the words of Panthea and in the description of the advancing spirits:

Look how the gusty sea of mist is breaking
In crimson foam, even at our feet! It rises
As ocean at the enchantment of the moon
Round foodless men wrecked on some oozy isle.

The fragments of the cloud are scattered up;
The wind that lifts them disentwines my hair:
The billows now sweep o'er mine eyes: my brain
Grows dizzy: I see thin shapes within the mist.

While the mule rested at Noë, the party walked to the rocky slopes beyond the meadows, and discovered a "pine forest" all carpeted with moss; and here one might see a multitude of young trees springing out of clefts in the stone, with shady retreats arranged under the fringe of drooping boughs. On returning to the inn they found that they were abandoned and betrayed: the moonstruck *voiturier* had departed alone, taking their baggage, and leaving word that he should expect to see them at Pontarlier, about twenty miles away. Sorely and painfully they crept along the road till the evening fell, Shelley with a sprained ankle and the ladies with aching limbs; but their spirit was high, and "the scenery," they said, "was lovely enough to beguile us of fatigue." We suppose that Shelley himself supplied the words of the description. "The hornèd moon hung in the light of sunset, that threw out a glow of unusual depth of redness over the piny mountains and the dark deep valleys: at intervals in the woods were beautiful lawns, interspersed with picturesque clumps of trees, and dark pines overshadowed our road." At Pontarlier they came up with the truant conductor, who stammered out his falsehoods and excuses: "and thus ended the adventures of that day."

TOUR OF 1814: SWITZERLAND AND THE RHINE

THE travellers were now fast approaching the frontier of Switzerland. In front of them stood the range of the Lower or Western Jura and the opening of the Valley of the Doubs, where the road wound onward through a gorge between high cliffs: "the scenery was divine, with piny mountains, barren rocks, and spots of verdure surpassing imagination." They crossed the frontier at Vervières, and descended for about three miles between overhanging woods, with green glades here and there interspersed, and lawns running upwards from the valley. At St. Sulpice they admired the trim *châlets*, much cleaner and neater than the French cottages. "The inhabitants," as they said, "exhibit the same contrast: the Swiss women wear a great deal of white linen, and their whole dress is always perfectly clean." Travellers in Germany, they had heard, have remarked the same difference between the Protestant and Catholic towns, and they were inclined to attribute the distinction to a variety in religion. There is an argument of much the same kind in Shelley's account of the Lake of Geneva. He contrasted the rude kingdom of Sardinia with the free republics of Switzerland, and found in the comparison an illustration of "the blighting mischiefs of despotism." Gray commented in one of his letters upon Rousseau's argument in praise of Geneva as compared with the poverty of Savoy. The poet had a wholesome contempt for the romance in which the argument appeared: he thought it more absurd than Amadis de Gaul, and would not have cared if all the "good characters" had been hanged in the third volume; but he was deceived into agreeing with an obviously unfair piece of reasoning. We are shown the city and its miniature dominions, the abode of peace and plenty, its gay crowd on the ramparts, the militia marching in good broadcloth, the bankers and merchants bustling towards 'Change; while out in the Duchy of Chablais one met only a few barefooted peasants, living in misery and squalor. "And all this," said Mr. Gray, "makes any person who is not blind sensible what a difference there is between the two Governments, that are the causes of the one view and the other."

Old Swiss Chalets.

The mule had now become very lame, and the travellers felt that the moods of the mad *voiturier* were no longer to be borne. "We determined to engage a horse," they said, "for the remainder of the way"; but they were anticipated; "he had determined to leave them at this village, and had taken measures to that effect." Their new guide was a young Swiss farmer, who pointed to the forest-lawns with glee, and vowed that they produced the finest cheese and butter in the world. The road led between the highest points of the mountain-range: the rocks overhung them above, and below were masses of trees, and a river reflecting the sun. The mountains were "so little asunder" that in time of war the ravine was closed by a chain. On the neck of the pass the Alpine ranges broke upon their view, and they saw beneath their feet the stony tract of Val Travers, the flats of Neuchâtel, and the shining expanses of the lake.

A carriage-drive to Lucerne occupied rather more than two days. They went by way of Soleure, and thought the whole journey extremely dull, except for occasional glimpses of the great chain of Alps in the distance. At the Lake of Lucerne they hoped for better things. They continually debated whether they should cross the St. Gothard, but were afraid of the expense; in any case, however, they would see the Painted Chapel on the spot where Tell's lime-tree stood, and the records of his vengeance against the oppressors of his country. They arrived at the town of Lucerne on the 23rd of August, and hired a boat at once, proposing to coast the lake in search of "some suitable habitation," or perhaps to push on to Altorf and make their way over the mountains into Italy. Shelley's condition of health was known to be precarious, and it was but a few months later that he was in actual danger :

> There late was one, within whose subtle being
> As light and wind within some delicate cloud
> That fades amid the blue noon's burning sky,
> Genius and Death contended.

Brunnen, after some hesitation, was selected as their temporary headquarters. The village stands near the opening of the Bay of Uri, a long reach lying at right angles to the main body of the lake: in front was the Painted Chapel, which the travellers were destined never to reach, and in the valley behind lay the peaceful town of Schwyz, with its "sweet fields" and meadows spreading "in unambitious compass." At Brunnen was a broken-down *château*, where rooms could be hired for a guinea a month; and here Shelley proposed to set up his abode, at least until they could make up their minds about an expedition into Italy. "The high mountains encompassed us," says the Journal, "darkening the waters"; the summits of several of the mountains were covered with eternal snow. "We remained," it was added, "on the shore of the lake, conversing, enjoying the rising breeze, and contemplating with feelings of exquisite delight the divine objects that surrounded us." When they became familiar with the beauties of Lake Leman in their later tour, they still remembered with regret the "sacred solitude and deep seclusion" which had so delighted them in their visit to Brunnen. Next day a fierce south-wind arose, and tore the lake into foam, shooting the water into spouts that fell back like a deluge of rain. The scene was well described by Mrs. Shelley in "Frankenstein": "I have visited the lakes of Lucerne and Uri, where the snowy mountains descend almost perpendicularly to the water, casting black and impenetrable shades, which would cause a gloomy and mournful appearance were it not for the verdant islands that relieve the eye. I have seen this lake agitated by a tempest when the wind tore up whirlwinds of water, and gave you an idea of what the waterspout must be on the great ocean." We know, too, that when Goethe's mind was full of the legends of this lake, and was already "humming his hexameters," he described a thunderstorm which swept over its surface from the depths of the mountains. "I saw it," he said, "in the light of the loveliest morning sun, a rejoicing and a life in wood and meadow." He was asked if the great description of sunrise in the second part of "Faust" was not founded on his recollections: and he answered, that, without the impression of those wonderful scenes, he could never have conceived the subject which he had touched in his "terza rima." "But that is all which I have coined from the gold of my Tell localities: the rest I left to Schiller, who, as we know, made the most beautiful use of it." On the abating of the storm, Shelley was so incautious as to sit in the evening on the wet pier, reading from Tacitus about the preparations for the siege of Jerusalem, the civic broils, the comet and the tempest of meteors, and the voices as of a multitude departing from the Holy City. Between the chance of illness and the certainty of money troubles, it was clear that they must make for home. Conveyance by water was cheap enough; and fortunately as they calculated, by taking advantage of barges on the Reuss and Rhine, they might reach England without travelling a league on land. From Lucerne to the Falls of Loffenburg they had places in the *diligence-par-eau:* between the Falls and Basle they

used the narrow punts which they called their
"Indian canoes." These were so alarmingly unsafe
that they tried once or twice to proceed by land,
hiring a return carriage that unluckily broke down,
and walking for some miles in the neighbourhood of
Rheinfelden. One delightful day was passed on a
barge laden with goods for Strasburg. There were
no other passengers, and Shelley read aloud the
"Letters from Sweden and Norway," by Mary Wollstonecraft, whose fine descriptions of scenery and
strength in narrative were emulated but never surpassed by her daughter, the authoress of "Frankenstein." The journey from Strasburg to Bonn may
be described in the words of that romance: "We
passed many willowy islands, and saw several
beautiful towns, and we stayed a day at Mannheim,
and on the fifth day arrived at Mayence. The course
of the Rhine below Mayence becomes much more
picturesque. The river descends rapidly, and winds
between hills, not high, but of beautiful forms. In
one spot you view rugged hills, ruined castles overlooking tremendous precipices, with the dark Rhine
rushing beneath; and on the sudden turn of a promontory, flourishing vineyards with green sloping
banks, and a meandering river and populous towns,
occupy the scene. We travelled at the time of the
vintage, and heard the song of the labourers as we

glided down the stream. Look at that castle which overhangs yon precipice; and that on the island, almost concealed amongst the foliage of those lovely trees; and now that group of labourers coming from among their vines, and that village half-hid in the recess of the mountain." Shelley himself, as Medwin has told us, used to dilate with an infectious enthusiasm " on the rapidity of their descent past terraced vineyards and castled heights ": on such a topic he seemed to be able "to intoxicate his imagination," and to lavish its inexhaustible store " with the prodigality of Nature in some tropical island." This part of the Rhine, says Mrs. Shelley, is that which was so beautifully described by Lord Byron in the Third Canto of " Childe Harold." That canto was written at the Villa Diodati in the summer of 1816, when the whole party were residing in the environs of Geneva. Lord Byron, we are told, was the only one who put his thoughts upon paper, while the fine weather continued; "these, as he brought them successively to us, clothed in all the light and harmony of poetry, seemed to stamp as divine the glories of heaven and earth." His companions read the verses with delight, as they conjured up memories of Stolzenfels and Ehrenbreitstein and the " breast of waters "

STOLZENFELS.

broadly swelling between the banks and crags of the winding Rhine :

> The negligently grand, the fruitful bloom
>   Of coming ripeness, the white city's sheen,
> The rolling stream, the precipice's gloom,
>   The forest's growth, and Gothic walls between
> The wild rocks shaped as they had turrets been
>   In mockery of man's art.

This part of the Rhine, said Mrs. Shelley, came to her remembrance as "the loveliest Paradise on earth." But when they had threaded the last narrows near Bonn, and had seen the end of the Seven Hills, they began to dread the idea of winding slowly through the sandy flats of Holland, and made up their minds to proceed by land to Rotterdam. They missed in their haste the pleasure of watching the splendid effects of dawn and sunset on what seems like a silver lake, and the peaceful charm of drifting past willowy shores and the wharves of the river-side towns, as Wordsworth has it :

> More perfect was the pleasure
> When hurrying forward, till the slackening stream
>   Spread like a spacious mere ; we then could measure
> A smooth free course along the watery gleam,
>   Think calmly on the past, and mark at leisure
> Features which else had vanished like a dream.

The travellers seem to have found nothing worth

remarking in the whole course of their journey by land. The slow diligence crawled in a long day over the eight leagues between Cologne and Cleves. For the drive to Rotterdam we must refer to a more lively report. "Sure nothing," says Lady Mary Wortley Montague, "can be more agreeable than travelling in Holland: the whole country appears a large garden; the roads are well paved, shaded on each side with rows of trees, and bordered with large canals full of boats passing and repassing. Every twenty paces gives you the prospect of some villa, and every four hours that of a large town, so surprisingly neat I am sure you would be charmed with them." Rotterdam, our travellers remarked, was wonderfully clean: "The Dutch even wash the outside brickwork of their houses." For the rest, they could find little to admire. The roads, they thought, were too narrow and sandy; the windmills too near the carriage-way; the flax drying against the treees had a disagreeable smell, and the canals were full of "enormous frogs and toads": "the only sight that refreshed the eye was the delicious verdure of the fields." It is curious to observe how closely the writer of the Journal noticed insects and reptiles. In the central plain of France she mentions the multitude of white butterflies that hovered about the chalky road; on the way to Besançon she tells us how "a thousand beautiful summer insects skimmed over the streams": at Geneva her attention is given at once to the chirping grasshoppers, the humming of sun-loving insects, the pleasure of relieving fallen cockchafers, and watching the motions of "a myriad of lizards." When they reached Nimeguen they had nothing to say about the size of the great church or the beauties of the sloping hill; but they mentioned the "turf-fortifications" and the flying-bridge over the Waal, which Lady Mary had described in her Letters. She had loved to linger among the ruins of the Walkenhof and the tall trees mirrored in the stream. She was reminded of Nottingham and the silver Trent, and declared that one has but to exchange the names of two rivers, "and there is no distinguishing the prospect." The houses in each case were built one above the other, and stood intermixed among trees and gardens. Julius Cæsar's Tower had much the same situation as Nottingham Castle. It is true, she admits, that the fortifications make a considerable difference: "All the learned in the art of war bestow great commendation upon them. For my part, I shall content myself with telling you 'tis a very pretty walk on the ramparts, on which there is a tower, very deservedly called the Belvidera, where people go to drink coffee and tea, and enjoy one of the finest prospects in the world." "I must not forget to take notice of the bridge, which appeared very surprising to me : it is large enough to hold hundreds of men, with horses and carriages ; they give the value of an English twopence to get upon it, and then away they go, bridge and all, to the other side of the river, with so slow a motion, one is hardly sensible of any at all." On the evening of the 8th of September, in the Journal called the 8th of August by mistake, Shelley and his party sailed from Rotterdam to the Thames, after being detained for two days at Maasluys, a little above the bar. Like Lady Mary in her yacht, they were "tossed very handsomely" in crossing; but they reached Gravesend on the third day after leaving the Dutch coast, "after an unexpectedly short navigation."

TOUR OF 1816: THE LAKE OF GENEVA

In the summer of 1816 the same trio took up their residence for about three months in the environs of Geneva. They reached Paris on the 8th of May, but were detained by some trouble about passports. The French Government had become more circumspect since the escape of the Comte de Lavalette, who had been condemned to death after Waterloo "as an accomplice in Buonaparte's treason"; but his guard had allowed him to slip out of prison in his wife's clothes, and he had been smuggled abroad about the beginning of January. The travellers made their way to Troyes by the route which they had followed two years before; but instead of taking the turn to Pontarlier, they proceeded by way of Dijon to Geneva. They passed Dôle without waiting for the view of Mont Blanc, which is visible from the hills though a hundred miles away. The foot of Jura was reached at Poligny, where the houses are overshadowed by a cliff that rises suddenly from the plain. "We proceeded," says the Journal, "by the light of a stormy moon to Champagnolles, in the depth of the mountains": the serpentine road clung on one side to the precipice, and the other side was "a gulf filled by the darkness of the driving clouds." The next day was spent in passing the forest, which filled the clefts of the valleys and wound high into the regions of frost. The snow fell fast, the sun occasionally breaking out and illuminating the deep ravines: as the evening advanced the storm was fiercer, and began to impede their way as they approached Les Rousses and the Swiss frontier. From Les Rousses there are two roads to Geneva: the one by Nion, in Swiss territory, the other by Gex, for which latter their passports had been arranged; the trifling difficulty was settled in the usual fashion. They hired four horses for Nion, with ten men to hold up the carriage, and left Les Rousses at six in the evening, the snow and darkness depriving them of the expected view of the Lake of Geneva and the Alps in the distance.

Near Geneva it was all sunshine again. They established themselves in the Hôtel de Londres at Sécheron, about a mile and a half from the city, and were joined there soon afterwards by Lord Byron, accompanied by Dr. Polidori and the rest of his suite. "We see the lovely lake, blue as the heavens which it reflects, and sparkling with golden beams": we are shown the smiling slopes of the Pays de Vaud, ridges of black mountains, and Mont Blanc in its majesty. Such is the view reflected by the lake. A few words out of Byron's Journal will show that the picture was not overcoloured. On July the 20th he writes: "I observed for some time the distinct reflection of Mont Blanc and Mont Argentière in the calm of the lake, while I was crossing in my boat: the distance of these mountains from their mirror is sixty miles." Shelley and Byron had joined in purchasing a little craft, in which they made constant expeditions. "You know our attachment to water-excursions. Every evening we sail on the lake, which is delightful, whether we glide over a glassy surface or are speeded along by a strong wind." The first letter is full of the gaiety of the spring. "I feel as happy as a new-fledged bird," says its writer, "and hardly care what twig I fly to, so that I may try my new-found wings." "We read Latin and Italian during the heats of noon." We know from other sources that Shelley during this year read Lucretius, Pliny's Letters, and the Annals and "Germany" of Tacitus; and we may conclude that he kept up the reading of Ariosto, Tasso, and Alfieri, which he had commenced not long before. The list of English works for the same year included "Paradise Lost," the "Faery Queen," and a translation of "Don Quixote." Later in the season, he tells us, the friends used to crowd round a blazing wood-fire at Montalègre or the Villa Diodati, amusing themselves with German ghost-stories; and it was from a playful competition in imitating those horrors that the romance of "Frankenstein" took its origin.

The next letter was written at the Campagne Chapuis, or Montalègre, near the Hill of Coligny, on the "Bellerive" or eastern shore of the lake. A small garden divided the cottage from the shore, and farther up the hill, across a vineyard, was Byron's "divine Diodati." They had exchanged the view of Mont Blanc for the dark-frowning Jura. The letter deplores a break-up of the weather and the torrents of an almost perpetual rain. "The thunderstorms that visit us are grander and more terrific than I have ever seen before: we watch them as they approach, observing the lightning play among the clouds in various parts of the heavens and dart in jagged figures upon the piny heights of Jura." One of these storms is described in "Frankenstein." The narrator is crossing the lake at night in order to reach Plainpalais, and during the short voyage he sees the pallid lightnings playing round the head of Mont Blanc in fantastic figures. The clouds seemed to advance very rapidly, and the thunder broke with a crash above him. "The storm, as is often the case in Switzerland, appeared at once in various parts of the heavens." The most violent commotion was exactly north of the town; another storm illumined the Jura with faint flashes; "and another darkened and sometimes disclosed the Môle, a peaked mountain to the east of the lake." Byron touches on the same subject in "Childe Harold," where he tells us how the lake was lit at night by phosphoric fires:

> And now the glee
> Of the loud hills shakes with its mountain-mirth,
> As if they did rejoice o'er a young earthquake's birth.

"The thunder-storms," he says, "to which these lines refer, occurred on the 13th of June 1816, at midnight; I have seen among the Acroceraunian mountains of Chimari several more terrible, but none more beautiful." We may see how the two poets were becoming accustomed to use a common store of images. We recognise Shelley's vision of Mont Blanc, where the old Earthquake-dæmon teaches lessons of ruin to her young, and his repeated allusions to the snows of Chimari and Arethusa's couch "in the Acroceraunian mountains"; and we shall find Byron in the same way borrowing from Shelley his metaphor of the "broken mirror," and weaving into "Manfred" the words which had first occurred to Shelley's mind in the Vale of Chamouni.

The description of Geneva is very imperfect, and there was an obvious mistake about Plainpalais. The writer of the letter supposed that this was the promenade where some of the Magistrates were murdered in the Revolution: this is situated within the walls, and is the place where a bust of Rousseau was set up. The promenade was abandoned in consequence of the massacre, and the citizens thenceforth resorted to Plainpalais, which extends its garden-like expanse from the city wall to the crags of Mont Salève. This letter contains a charming description of the vine-dressers' songs. "The theme of their ballads consists of shepherds, love, flocks, and the sons of kings who fall in love with beautiful shepherdesses. Their tunes are monotonous, but it is sweet to hear them in the stillness of evening, while we are enjoying the sight of the setting sun, either from the hill behind our house or from the lake."

The tour of the lake is described by Shelley himself in a letter to Thomas Love Peacock. This letter bears the date of July the 12th and the address of Montalègre, but with the exception of a few lines at the end it had been written at Vevey nearly a fortnight before. It contains an abstract of the whole voyage, which, as he said, lasted eight days, "and if you have a map of Switzerland, you can follow me." Shelley and Byron started in their boat from Montalègre at half-past two in the afternoon of June the 23rd; on Saturday, the 30th, they quitted Ouchy, "and after two days' pleasant sailing arrived at Montalègre on Sunday evening." It seems that neither Shelley nor Byron had ever studied the "Nouvelle Héloise," which had been written many years before either of them was born. They now read it for the first time, and found that in some parts it formed an excellent guide-book. The travellers threw themselves with zeal into an attempt to identify the very places where its imaginary incidents might have occurred; and they were probably unaware at the time that its author had admitted the existence of topographical errors and transpositions of scenery, in some cases due to carelessness and in others to a desire to lead the reader astray. There was something about the book which fascinated Shelley for a time, even while he disagreed with its sentiments; but in the "Triumph of Life" he placed its author among those who fell disgraced in the Valley of Oblivion: "I have suffered what I wrote, and viler pain, and so my words have seeds of misery." The matter has long ceased to be important, but Meillerie is still "enchanted ground," even if Rousseau were "no magician." Shelley's letter contains a series of miniature sketches, bold in outline and infused with a delicate brightness. He touches lightly on the traditions received from the villagers and boatmen; it would be useless to expect any discussion of their historical value. A three-hours' row brought the strangers to a ruined tower, which was reported to have been built by Cæsar, when he shut in the Helvetians with his famous Wall; and it seems that there had been three more of these "towers of Julius," which the men of Geneva had used as quarries when they fortified their town "*alla moderna.*" The neighbouring town of Hernance had grown up round "a great hall of Burgundy"; it was founded ages ago by a Queen of the Barbarians, and had been reduced to ruin by the armies of Berne, "who burnt and ravaged everything they could find." In the evening the tourists arrived at Nerni, and they noticed as they paced the beach how the line of "the purple and misty waters" was broken by two craggy islands near the shore.

Shelley stood by the waterside and watched the fish sporting on the surface and crowding up to catch the insects that fell from the rocks. Lake Leman is celebrated for its "Umbla," or *Ombre*, for the pike at the outlet of the Rhone, and the giant lake-trout known as *truite saumonnée*. Byron might remember the supper provided for Walpole and Gray: for he was in correspondence with old Mr. Bonstetten, who remembered Gray as "the most melancholy and gentlemanlike of all possible poets." "One night," the pensive poet had written, "we ate part of a trout taken in the lake that weighed thirty-seven pounds: they assured us that it was not uncommon to catch them of fifty pounds. They are dressed here, and sent to Paris on some great occasions—nay, even to Madrid, as we were told." The fish that Shelley observed were probably of the kind called *ferra*, looking like something between a white-trout and a herring. This is, indeed, shown by their being classed as *Coregonus Clupeoides*. They are hardly to be distinguished from the "gwyniad" of Lake Bala, in North Wales, and the "skellies" of Ulleswater. Alexandre Dumas, who knew all about gastronomy, has warned travellers that the *ferra* should be served with the white wine of Vevey; and he declared that it was as good as the *lavalet* of Neuchâtel, and almost as delicate as the shads that ascend the Seine in spring-time.

After walking up to the village, the visitors saw the children playing at Genevan bowls, which somewhat resembled "curling" on dry land, or at least had borrowed some incidents from "the roaring game." The party looked out for a very uneven ground: the first hand threw his bowl so as to rest where it struck: "if that be a fortunate situation, the next player pitches his bowl directly upon his adversary, so as to make it spring away, while his own fixes itself in the spot." Most of the children had their throats enlarged by *goître*, which argued something wrong with the water-supply. The disease is very local; it is said that it existed in those days only in one hamlet of the Vale of Chamouni; but it was admitted, on the other hand, that there was an idiot in almost every family. Some of the peasants, before tourists abounded, would have been glad to change places with the *cretins*. "*Ils sont très heureux,*" said an old soldier to Dr. Moore: "if I had been one I should not have had to work." "Would you take a *goître*," said the Doctor, "to be quit of rates and taxes?" "*Très volontiers, monsieur,*" was the reply: "the one is just as good as the other."

The evening was spent in conversation about Greece and the Islands. A servant had brightened up the rooms, but the place still looked somewhat disconsolate. Byron said that it was like the rough parts of the Morea—"it is five years since I have slept in such a bed"; and he described his wanderings in 1810-11, when he visited the Pasha at Tripolitza, and made a tour by Napoli di Romania and Argos.

As they rounded the promontory in the morning the lake assumed a wilder aspect. The mountains fell in broken ridges towards a broad bay; the pine-woods made a dark band between the icy rocks aloft in the blue air and the groves of oak and chestnut with "lawny fields" near the shore. The next bay fronted the marshy plain formed by the divided streams of the Drance, a glacier-torrent which dashes down through lofty glens and squanders itself in an expanse of sand and mud. The shallows teem with fish, and are haunted by coots and crested grebes and a multitude of shore-birds, for which the boatmen find quaint names in their *patois*. The curlew is a "*crenet*"; the sandpipers are distinguished by their cries, as the "*sifflet*," the "*sifflasson*," and the "*tiou-tiou*"; and there is a "*bécassine*" with a note very different from the bleating of an English snipe. The entrances of the river were crowded with "*besolets*," or black-hooded terns, standing by the streams or "winnowing up and down" in a gull-like flight. "There were thousands of these *besolets*," said Shelley; "beautiful water-birds, like sea-gulls, but smaller, and with purple on their backs."

The weather broke as they left the bay: a rainy

squall from the east was followed by a hot blast from the south: the wind seemed to be in all quarters, and there was "thunder out of a clear sky," such as terrified the Roman poet. "During our voyage," remarks Shelley, "on the distant height of a hill, we saw a ruined castle, which reminded me of those on the Rhine." In the evening they put up at Evian-les-Bains, which was even then a fashionable resort. There are alkaline waters, said to be useful for the gout, and the rich citizens of Geneva used to come over for the cure, or to amuse themselves in a delightful retreat. The town is situated on the old Roman road near a plain "flanked with fine tall trees": there was a large and well-dressed company; but Shelley, being in a desponding mood, could see nothing that was even tolerable. "The appearance of the inhabitants," he wrote, "is more wretched, diseased, and poor than I ever recollect to have seen."

A stormy passage brought the boat to Meillerie, sailing in the shadow of mighty forests, under mountains "with icy points," rising straight above the cliffs whose base was "echoing to the waves." A torrent foamed through the gorge between a fir-wood and clumps of oak trees: in the background stood the cliffs of the Dent d'Oche, shutting out the sight of the crest of ice, that covered it "in the beginning of the world." The visitors took pains to identify the exact places connected with the old romance, just as at Clarens they were pleased at being shown the place of the "visionary woods" and disturbed at the "brutal outrage" which had obliterated their imaginary growth. Rousseau, said Byron, was unfortunate about his "local habitations." "The Prior of Great St. Bernard has cut down some of his woods for the sake of a few casks of wine;" and Buonaparte had levelled part of the rocks of Meillerie in improving the Simplon route. The road was an excellent piece of work; but the poet could hardly agree with the remark made in his presence, that "*La route vaut mieux que les souvenirs.*"

Both Byron and Shelley have left accounts of the dangerous squall in which their boat was nearly capsized. "I had the fortune," said the former, "good or evil as it might be, to sail from Meillerie, where we landed for some time, to St. Gingoux during a lake-storm, which added to the magnificence of all around, although occasionally accompanied by danger to the boat, which was small and overloaded." Shelley's account is far more highly coloured. The waves, he writes, were of a frightful height, and they covered the whole surface with "a chaos of foam." The boatman was slow in releasing the sheet, and the waves began to come in. Byron, of course, was an excellent swimmer. "He took off his coat," says Shelley, "I did the same, and we sat with our arms crossed, every instant expecting to be swamped." Shelley's courage was indomitable, as appears from several incidents of his life, and it is therefore the more interesting to learn what his feelings were when his life, as he thought, was in peril "from the immensity of the waves." " I felt in this near prospect of death a mixture of sensations, among which terror entered, though subordinately. My feelings would have been less painful had I been alone: but I know that my companion would have attempted to save me, and I was overcome with humiliation when I thought that his life might have been risked to preserve mine." Knowing what happened afterwards behind the sea-fog and under a black cloud in the Gulf of Spezia, must we not feel that in these words we have a glimpse of his actual fate, as if we saw the darkness opened and Shelley courageous in death? It seemed, said Trelawny, after the bodies had been found, that he probably went down at once, "for he was unable to swim, and had always declared that in case of wreck he would vanish instantly, and not imperil others in the endeavour to save him."

St. Gingoux was even more beautiful than Meillerie.

The mountains are higher, and they descend "more abruptly" to the lake. "On high the aërial summits still cherish great depths of snow in their ravines and in the paths of their unseen torrents." The forests, we are told, seemed to have become deeper: "the chestnut gives a peculiarity to the scene, which is most beautiful, and will make a picture in my memory." They saw a huge tree which had been overthrown by the storm earlier in the day; and Byron in his "Childe Harold" added a note to the same effect: "We found that the wind had been sufficiently stormy to blow down some fine old chestnut trees on the lower parts of the mountains." They now looked out upon the mouths of the Rhone, where a line of "tremendous breakers" marked its confluence with the lake. The turbid waters seemed to mix unwillingly with the "azured crystal," as if fearing to soil its purity; yet when they looked around they perceived that the whole expanse between the shores had been formed as a channel for such a river to fill. Shelley reverted to the phrase more than once when he was passing through the ravine "which is at once the couch and the creation of the Arve."

As Byron always rose late, his companion had time for a long visit to the waterfalls above St. Gingoux. The whole river was but a chain of cataracts, whirling between the caverned rocks, and drenching the foliage with a perpetual spray. The **path sometimes** left the rocky banks and deviated into meadows and pastures : " and in these meadows," said Shelley, " I gathered a nosegay of such flowers as I never saw in England."

Being as yet no botanist, Shelley gave us no details as to the particular kinds that he admired. If exact information were required, it might be conveniently found in Ray's list of the plants in this neighbourhood. " Our long stay at Geneva," said the traveller, " and that in the proper season for ' simpling ' **gave us leisure to** search for and advantage in finding many species **of** plants in the neighbouring fields and mountains "; and he adds a list of all the " simples," unknown or rarely found at home, which he observed near the streams and in the woods, and generally in the zone of vegetation from the lake to the summit of Mont Salève.

The poet was up with the day, as if, like his own **figure of the** morning breeze, he were fed with " dews and sunrise "; the boatmen were lounging about the pier, and the craft lay idle and waiting:

> What think you, as she lies in her green cove,
> Our little sleeping boat is thinking of?
> If morning dreams are true, why I should guess
> That she was dreaming of our idleness,
> And of the miles of watery way
> **We** should have led her by this time of day !

"After breakfast we sailed for Clarens, determining first to see the three mouths of the Rhone, and then the Castle of Chillon." The day was fine and the water calm. Byron is seen entering in fine spirits, excited perhaps at what he thought to be an early start:

> The morn is up again, the dewy morn,
>   With breath all incense and with cheek all bloom,
> Laughing the clouds away with playful scorn,
>   And living as if earth contained no tomb,
> And glowing into day: we may resume
>   The march of our existence.

Sailing to Chillon, they looked toward the head of the lake, and saw the white houses of Villeneuve crowding about the shore, the tower of La Bouverie under the cliff, the huge mountains of the Oberland "clothed in clouds," and the willowy plain of the Valais. In describing the castle we shall follow Byron's account in the main. It is situated between the towns of Villeneuve and Clarens, in Montreux; on the left are the entrances of the Rhone, and beyond them the heights above Meillerie and St. Gingoux. The neighbouring districts of the Pays de Vaud were inhabited by the descendants of the Protestant refugees from Piedmont and Savoy, and in the times of persecution the prisons at Chillon were filled with the supporters of the Reformed doctrine. Close to the walls the water is said to be eight hundred feet deep; and Byron adopted even a more imposing measure :

> A thousand feet in depth below
> Its massy waters meet and flow;
> Thus much the fathom line was sent
> From Chillon's snow-white battlement.

Behind the castle there is a torrent, leaping down "channelled rocks," to which Byron paid another visit a few weeks afterwards. His journal gives us an entertaining account of the noisy or drunken gendarme who had shown them the black gallows-beam and the deep cells that might be flooded in a moment. He was just like Blücher, says Byron, "and to my mind as great a man." He seems, indeed, to have told the visitors nothing about the famous Bonnivard, of whom they only heard afterwards from friends at Geneva. Shelley mentions no date earlier than 1670 in connection with the prison, and adds that the names carved on the pillars were doubtless those of the prisoners, "of whom now no memory remains." In the year 1513 François de Bonnivard held office as " Prieur de St. Victor" at Geneva. It was mainly owing to his efforts that the city was not joined to Savoy under an agreement between the Bishop and the Duke. Bonnivard faced his enemies successfully for several years, but was captured at last, though travelling under the ducal safe-conduct, and was sent to the "living grave" at Chillon. For about two years he lay in the upper dungeon without any pretence of trial. Then the Duke visited the place, and ordered him to be cast into the vault of the seven columns, below the level of the lake. Released in 1536, during the war between Savoy and Berne, he became a citizen and councillor under the new constitution of Geneva. His advice was always in favour of moderation, and he even succeeded in checking the zeal of the followers of Calvin. He served his country like a hero, and wrote its history "with the *naïveté* of the philosopher and the enthusiasm of a patriot." The last of his good deeds was not the least; for he made a gift to the city of his precious collection of early-printed books, which became the foundation of its celebrated public library.

Such a man, wrote Byron, was worthy of the best age of freedom; and the "sad floor of Chillon" becomes an altar in his sonnet, "for 'twas trod, until his very steps have left a trace, by Bonnivard." But when he first visited the place in company with Shelley they knew as little about the patriot as Victor Hugo's tourist who boasted at the Hotel on the Rigi, "*J'ai visité Chillon, où est mort Bolivar!*" Byron may have repaired all omissions on his second arrival; but Dumas makes up too good a story about the stealthy movements of the "Pilgrim of Eternity." A boat glides like a swan below the castle-wall: there is a pale-faced man in a long black cloak, halting slightly as he stepped on the shore: " he demanded to see the dungeon of Bonnivard, and stayed there a long time alone, and when the guardians entered the vault again, they found the word 'Byron' carved on the rock where the martyr had been chained." It is, however, generally believed that the inscription is an impudent forgery.

The guides at Clarens were not much better than their colleague in the *château*. They chattered about Rousseau, and continually mixed up the man and his book. The visitors joined the haymakers under the legendary trees; and it was not until the next day that they discovered how they had been deceived about the "Bosquet." The *château* at Clarens was "a square strong house," surrounded by a double terrace, and approached by a steep road lined with walnut and chestnut: as they roamed in the deserted garden they picked roses for absent friends; but on Byron's later visit he found the terraces closed, and "the roses were gone with their summer."

Vevey, their next resting-place, is described as most beautiful in its simplicity: "its market-

place looks directly upon the mountains of Savoy and the Valais, the lake, and the valley of the Rhone." It was here that Byron stood gazing at the Alps, "in the very eyes of Mont Blanc," when he heard an English voice, and the question, "Did you ever see anything so rural?" Here, while lodging at "Le Cerf," the philosopher of Geneva had long ago composed his romance: and here, under the excitement of that tradition, Shelley wrote all but the concluding lines of his brilliant description of the lake.

They were detained at Ouchy by stress of weather, but took an opportunity of visiting Gibbon's house at Lausanne. We find in his Life an account of its delightful situation. "Communicating with the town on the north side, the south opened to a garden of the extent of four acres, ornamented by the taste of M. Deyverdun, where the cloudless sun of summer was only shaded by the lovely green of the groves of acacias." From the garden to the lake the whole country was covered with meadows and vineyards, interspersed here and there with villas and picturesque *châlets*. "We were shown," writes Shelley, "the decayed summer-house where he finished his History, and the old acacias on the terrace from which he saw Mont Blanc after having written the last sentence." We shall quote the very words of the historian: "It was on the day, or rather night, of the 27th of June 1787, between the hours of eleven and twelve, that I wrote the last lines of the last page in a summer-house in my garden. After laying down my pen, I took several turns in a *berceau* or covered walk of acacias, which commands a prospect of the country, the lake, and the mountains. The air was temperate, the sky was serene, the silver orb of the moon was reflected from the waters, and all nature was silent. I will not dissemble the first emotions of joy on the recovery of my freedom, and perhaps the establishment of my fame." The sudden departure of his cherished and accustomed toil, added Shelley, must have left him, like the death of a dear friend, sad and solitary. He does not notice the coincidence of the anniversary, which Byron evidently had in his mind. Byron wrote that evening to Mr. Murray: "I enclose you a sprig of Gibbon's acacia and some rose-leaves from his garden, which, with part of his house, I have just seen: you will find honourable mention in his Life made of this acacia, when he walked out on the night of concluding his History: the garden and summer-house, where he composed, are neglected, and the last utterly decayed."

During the one interval of sunshine in a stormy day, Shelley walked down to the pier, to watch the waves. "A rainbow spanned the lake, or rather rested one extremity of its arch upon the water, and the other at the foot of the mountains of Savoy: some white houses, I know not if they were those of Meillerie, shone through the yellow fire." We are reminded of the "sphere-fires" above the moist earth, and the marvellous imagery of "The Cloud":

> From cape to cape, with a bridge-like shape,
>   Over a torrent sea,
> Sunbeam-proof, I hang like a roof,
>   The mountains its columns be.
> The triumphal arch through which I march
>   With hurricane fire and snow,
> When the powers of the air are chained to my chair
>   Is the million-coloured bow.

TOUR OF 1816: CHAMOUNI

SHELLEY's second letter to Peacock was written piecemeal in the form of a diary. Its first portion, dated the 22nd of July 1816, contains an account of the journey from Geneva to Chamouni: two days afterwards, its writer added a description of the ice-cave at the source of the Arveiron, and of a visit to the Glacier des Bossons; the entries for July the 25th contain the wonderful pictures of Montanvert and the Mer de Glace; and the whole Journal concludes on the 28th with the return of the party to Montalègre. We should note the classical and stately style of the opening passage, which resembles Pliny's Letters in the facility shown in moulding language into new forms for thought. "Whilst you, my friend, are engaged in securing a home for us, we are wandering in search of recollections to embellish it." How could any one describe the wonders of the surrounding scene? He has read the raptures of travellers, and must be warned by their example. "To exhaust the epithets which express the astonishment and the admiration, the very excess of satisfied astonishment, where expectation scarcely acknowledged any boundary—is this to impress upon your mind the images which fill mine now even till it overflow?"

The first stage of the journey took them only to the gateway of the Alps. The day was cloudless, and the two ladies found the heat very oppressive. The ancient boundary of the Republic was reached a little more than a mile from the city wall, the territories of Savoy beginning at the brook of Chêne, and extending as far as the Great St. Bernard. The face of the country rises gradually from the base of Mont Salève to the Môle; though the soil is chiefly composed of sand and *débris*, it seemed to the travellers to be sufficiently fertile, and was at any rate covered with corn-fields and orchards. After passing the ravine of the Ménoge torrent the road mounted to the plateau of Nangy and Contamines, the latter village lying huddled up between the Arve and a hill that joins the Môle. A little farther on they passed under a steep escarpment of rock on which stood the ruins of the castle of Faucigny, once the head of that great lordship which included Mont Blanc and the Valley of Chamouni, Bonneville, Cluses, and Sallanches, and many other thriving towns and villages. Those who have read the earlier books on the Alps will remember that Mont Blanc and its companions were long without particular names, and were known in a general phrase as the *Montagnes Maudites* or the *Glacières du Faucigny*. These names were applied to the whole *cordon* between the Dent du Midi and the Great St. Bernard; but Mont Blanc was singled out as "*la Montagne Maudite*" in a special sense, as being a region known only to wild beasts and birds of prey, "where the stiffened corpse of Nature was lying in a winding-sheet." Shelley seems to have been thinking of this when he described the abode of the Earthquake-dæmon:

> A desert peopled by the storms alone,
> Save where the eagle brings some hunter's bone,
> And the wolf tracks her there. How hideously
> Its shapes are heaped around, rude, bare, and high,
> Ghastly and scarred and riven.

Bonneville was the capital of Faucigny before the lordship became an appendage of Dauphiné, at least after the burning of Cluses, at the beginning of the fourteenth century. When the travellers reached this point, they found that the peak or pyramid of the Môle had completely lost its accustomed shape, and stood over the Arve in a frowning ridge. On the other side of the narrow defile rises the Brezon, with a steep face of cliff fronting the town, and green terraces sloping on each side towards the stream. The two mountains form a kind of gateway into the higher Alps, but there is nevertheless a great gap beside the Môle, where a huge mountain seems to have fallen in ruin :

> Mountains have fallen,
> Leaving a gap in the clouds, and with the shock
> Rocking their Alpine brethren : filling up
> The ripe green valleys with destruction's splinters,
> Damming the rivers with a sudden dash,
> Which crushed the waters into mist, and made
> Their fountains find another channel.   Thus,
> Thus in its old age did Mount Rosenberg.

Shelley mentions another celebrated instance. Mont d'Anterne, a high mountain near Servoz, began to fall on a certain Sunday in 1751. The dust rose in black clouds like columns of smoke, and it was reported at Turin that a terrible volcano had broken out. The King of Sardinia at once despatched Vitaliano Donati, a famous Venetian naturalist, to report on the nature of the disaster. Donati was in time to see a great part of the fall, and was able to trace it to the action of water percolating from certain lakes, and to an abnormal fall of snow, as may be seen in the works of De Saussure.

On leaving Bonneville the next morning the tourists passed a fine stone bridge across the Arve, and shortly afterwards entered the marshy valley of Cluses, not so fertile as Shelley supposed; a new road led across the fields, and there was a fine view of mountains on all sides. Above the heights crowned with pine and chestnut they could see the snow-peaks of the Morche and the Dent du Midi. After a time, when the valley became narrow, the road seemed to be forced by the river against the side of the mountain. M. Leschevin of Geneva, who wrote very shortly before that time, left an interesting account of this part of the route. The road was shaded by oaks and walnut-trees, and led the traveller through the greenest of pastures. After leaving the slopes of the Môle he descended into the flat valley near Siongy, where stood the fine house that had been the Chartreuse of the Reposoir, and where once had been a tall belfry, destroyed by a fanatical deputy in a wild crusade against steeples. Here the travellers were but half a league from Cluses, though nothing of the town could be seen. There was a *cirque* or amphitheatre of cliffs, enclosing a tract of meadows and oak-woods, without any apparent opening: then the road turned suddenly to the right, and crossed the river, and they looked down into a little arcaded town nestled up against an enormous precipice.

This little town of watchmakers had a somewhat amusing history. The military importance of its site had made it an object of favour to its ancient lords. The inhabitants were permitted to fortify their town and to practise the use of arms. Though not exactly noble, the men of Cluses were free to hold fiefs and lordships, and were exempt from tolls in all the markets of Savoy. It is said that they once destroyed an army by rolling down stones from their heights; it is certain that they were bold enough to burn Bonneville, after their own town was destroyed, and to bring back a number of captured serfs to help in restoring their home. There was a Marquis, who called himself their feudal lord; but his only privilege was to have the tongue when a beast was killed. The Porter of Cluses was a much greater man, for he was not only the Executioner, but also Colonel of the Guard. The greatest of all was the "Abbot of Basoche," otherwise known as the Knight of the Popingay. Every year they had a *Fête Patriotique*, or Wappenshaw, in which noblemen from a distance were glad to join. A wooden bird was set on a rock, and the successful marksman, who knocked the prize from its perch, at once became King of the Feast and Mayor of the Town, whose duty was to create a new burgess, and to open the ball in the evening with the queen whom he had decked with a rose.

The name of Cluses is derived from the gorge in which the cliffs almost meet. "They press so closely on the town," Dr. Moore wrote, about 1780, "that when I stood in the principal street, each end of it appeared to be perfectly shut up; and wherever any of the houses had fallen down, the vacancy was plugged up in the same manner by a green mountain." Sir Frederick Eden wrote home a few years later: "The mountains almost appear to close; then they open into spacious valleys, and every now and then we catch a glimpse of the distant Alps and the snowy head of Mont Blanc." The savage and colossal gorge of Cluses reminded Shelley of Derbyshire. "The scene," he says, "differs from Matlock only in its immense proportions and inaccessible solitude." Mrs. Shelley discussed the same idea in her romance. The country near Matlock in her opinion resembled this part of Switzerland; "but everything is on a lower scale, and the green hills want the crown of white Alps which attend on the piny mountains." They had visited "the wondrous cave," which might well be compared to the legend-haunted "Caverne du Balme," and the little Cabinet of Natural History, "where the curiosities are disposed in the same manner as in the collections at Servoz and Chamouni." All through this part of the journey Shelley talked of home: he compared an innkeeper's little museum to what he had seen at the lakes or Bethgelert, and the trays of curious minerals at Chamouni to the specimens at Keswick and Matlock and Clifton. A passage in Mrs. Shelley's book seems to refer to a conversation upon this point. "A tingling long-lost sense of pleasure often came across me during the journey to Mont Blanc: some turn in the road, some new object, suddenly perceived and recognised, reminded me of days gone by, and were associated with the light-hearted gaiety of boyhood."

As the road goes from Balme towards Magland the valleys open into those lawns embowered in green leaves which M. Bourrit described with such artistic enthusiasm. "The ravishing vision enchants me, and follows me wherever I go. The emerald sward is watered by the river below and shaded by tall trees above: it is the theatre of my imagination, and I can only pity and smile at the traveller who thinks that he enjoys it as he trots by on his mule or lies ensconced in his *berline*." Shortly after the road left the rich and beautiful village of Magland the travellers walked up to see the cascade of the Nant d'Arpenaz, where a crystal brook falls into the valley over a cliff about 800 feet high. Shelley, it may be observed, adds half as much again to its proper height, and makes the same mistake with respect to the neighbouring cascade of the " Egyptian Statue." " The violence with which it fell," he remarks, " made it look more like some shape which an exhalation had assumed than like water, for it streamed beyond the mountain, which appeared dark behind it." It is interesting to observe how almost similar phrases may be used to produce contrary effects. The waterfalls of the Lotos-eaters, for instance, were taken by Tennyson from what he had seen in the Pyrenees. In Shelley's picture the evanescent cloud of spray floats upwards across the black rock, and the fleecy foam of the lesser fall rolls down upon the sculptured stone; but the stream in the Lotos-land slants towards the earth like mist before the wind, and the heavy veil floats like a fine " cloth of tiffany," more suited to the climate of the South:

> And like a downward smoke the slender stream
> Along the cliffs to fall, and pause and fall, did seem.
> A land of streams ! Some, like a downward smoke,
> Slow-dropping veils of thinnest lawn, did go;
> And some through wavering lights and shadows broke,
> Rolling a slumbrous sheet of foam below.

All the way from the Nant d'Arpenaz to St. Martin the cliffs on the left side are broken into a line of battlements, with cones of slaty rock, which take a fine purple colour as the sun goes down.

St. Martin, where Shelley's party rested for the night, is divided by a bridge from Sallanches, a busy place, of which the other village forms an unprosperous suburb. Our travellers did not cross the river, and may not have known of the fine view of Mont Blanc to be seen above the town. There is a green hexagonal hill behind Sallanches, with a ring of sharp rocks near the summit where the Dôme is seen far above the clouds. We read in Sir Frederick Eden's journal how he was taken there by Maxime the æsthetic guide, who was called "le Baron de la Pierre Ronde": "the setting sun produced a fine appearance on Mont Blanc, which looked like a sugar-loaf, and was tinged perfectly pink: had I not seen it in the morning, I should never have guessed that it was covered with snow."

On the morning of the 22nd of July the party proceeded by what was known as the "Grande Route" to the valley of Servoz. The road was in many places blocked with sand and stones brought down by the Arve, the bed of the track torn up, and the bridges damaged in the floods. It has long been replaced by the modern carriage-road, which leads from Sallanches, past the Bonnant and the ruins of St. Gervais, and meets the old track a little beyond the Pont Pélissier. In earlier times travellers had to force their way by a stony track along the heights of Passi, where a number of Roman remains, including two valuable inscriptions, show the line of the ancient trade-route across the Salassian territories. The difficulties of this route appear in the records of Pococke's expedition, and we can imagine the confusion that prevailed among his crowd of armed attendants in charge of the tents and baggage. "From Sallanches," he says, "the road began to be stony and rough, and we were obliged, not without danger, to wade through several brooks and wood-waters that fall from the rocks. In this manner, and with great difficulty, we got to Servoz, a poor village: there we were obliged to pass along the stony foot of a mountain, and at last we arrived at a long valley from which we descried the ice-mountains."

The hillside of Passi, with its orchards and hay-fields, and the sharp needle of Mont Varens in the sky, looked almost artificially designed, like a scene in a play. Two narrow pinnacles in front were reared like masts against the sky, and the clouds fell round them in folds, as if a huge ship were spreading her sails to the wind. "On the other side," says the theatrical Bourrit, "you have another *coup d'œil* for the stage"; but we must remember that he was a professional musician, and had an eye to operatic

MONT BLANC, FROM LAC DE CHÈDE.

effects. On arriving at the little village of Chède, nearly opposite to St. Gervais, all travellers were expected to mount a steep path that leads to a cascade and a miniature lake. An immense body of water dashed between the rocks, and cast a spray which formed a mist around it: "in the midst of it hung a multitude of sun-bows, which faded or became unspeakably vivid as the inconstant sun shone through the clouds." The rainbow seemed to form a perfect circle, perhaps twenty feet in diameter. We find an excellent description of its appearance in "Manfred." Lord Byron says: "This iris is formed by the rays of the sun over the lower parts of the Alpine torrents: it is exactly like a rainbow come down to pay a visit, and so close that that you may walk into it. This effect lasts till noon:

> It is not noon, the sun-bow's rays still arch
> The torrent with the many hues of heaven,
> And roll the sheeted silver's waving column
> O'er the crag's headlong perpendicular.

The little Lac de Chède, so well known by Bourrit's descriptions and drawings, and by the fine picture which the Republic of Geneva presented to M. Necker, is hardly more than a clear pool filled by a trickling rivulet; but the snowy Alps were reflected in its mirror, and there were tall trees drooping over mossy rocks and "velvet lawns." It does not follow from Shelley's omission to describe the mountain-pool that he left the lawns of Chède unobserved. We have already noticed his enjoyment of "the dells of lawny expanse," and in the Vale of Servoz he noticed openings in the forest "with lawns of such verdure as he had never seen before." In that fragment of an Essay on the Coliseum which was expected "to rival, if not to surpass, Corinne," Shelley compared the foliage on the arches to the lawny dells of soft short grass among the precipices of the Alps of Savoy. Medwin quotes another passage in which the ruin itself is likened to the ravine near Chamouni, as though "a nurseling of man" had been transformed by enchantment into a creation of Nature. The water falling from its broken ledges sounds like the voice of a stream in the forest: "changed to a mountain, cloven with woody dells and shattered into toppling precipices, even the clouds intercepted by its summits supply eternal fountains with their rain."

Shelley was fond of natural history, and within a few months after his return to England he gave considerable attention to anatomy, and became "a tolerable botanist." He was much interested in the collection of mineral specimens which Joseph Deschamps, the innkeeper at Servoz, had got together under the instructions of M. Jurine and other men of science at Geneva. Shelley mentions Servoz as a place " where there are lead and copper mines "; and it is true that the village long formed the headquarters of a French company that worked the minerals of Upper Faucigny. They found copper and silver-lead in this neighbourhood, besides some rich beds of iron-ore ; and it was said that they made steel as good as any at Sheffield or Langres, and that their copper in bars was highly esteemed by the watchmakers of Geneva and Cluses. The undertaking seems never to have been very profitable. The company had spent nearly a million francs at Servoz before 1791 ; and at that date they were only working at Foully, under Mont Chatelard, at the western end of the Valley of Chamouni. When the Revolution broke out, the directors emigrated, and the whole business came to an end. The neighbourhood of Servoz, however, continued to be famous for mineral specimens. M. Leschevin refers for their description to the *Journal des Mines*, No. 5 (1795). Besides the black, gray, and red hornblendes, and one or two stray deposits of gypsum and slate among the primitive rocks, he mentions the fine pink crystals of feldspar, a white fluor containing fibres of silver and copper, and pyrites containing copper and gold. He added a piece of advice for tourists, which no one was likely to adopt: "Go to the mountains and get the specimens for yourselves; for though Deschamps is an excellent fellow, *il vend un peu cher ses coquilles.*"

"We saw in this cabinet," says Shelley, "some chamois' horns, and the horns of an exceedingly rare animal called the *bouquetin*, which inhabits the deserts of Mont Blanc." This was the ibex, a mountain-goat, which Shelley classified by mistake as "a kind of deer." The hunters called it "ibsch" or "stein-bock." It is believed that a few of these animals remain on Mont Iséran, where they are strictly preserved by the King of Italy; but in Switzerland, Savoy, and the Tyrol the species is said to be extinct. We hear a good deal about the ibex in the Swiss literature of the seventeenth century. In Plantin's "Helvetia," for example, we are told that the animal can only live among the highest Alps, and would become blind in any warmer climate; that the oldest bucks have as many as twenty ridges on their curved horns; and that when the "ibsch" is about to die he clinches his horns round a peak, and twists himself round and round, until he grinds down the edge of those "anchored hooks," and falls dying into the gulf below. Ray has given us a charming account of a visit to the museum at Glarus in 1665: "Here we saw the horns of the ibex, which they call stein-bock, somewhat like goats' horns, only larger. The people said that the animal was long extinct in that neighbourhood, but that specimens might be found in the Valais or in the Archbishopric of Salzburg. They had plenty of chamois, which Ray calls "gimpses," and "of the Alpine mice, or marmottoes, they had a good store." M. Bourrit saw herds of ibex on the range of Mont Blanc upon more than one occasion. He describes a herd that he saw in 1781 when crossing the Col de la Seigne to Courmayeur. "This part of the Alps," he said, "is the Paradise of these peaceful creatures," and there were such ice-firths and labyrinths and "pathless Belvederes" that he could not believe that the breed would ever be destroyed. Shelley saw the huge ibex-horns both at Servoz and Chamouni; he described them as "broad, massy, pointed at the ends, and surrounded with a number of rings"; but they are more accurately described as being square-fronted, and marked with transverse ridges and knobs, which indicate the animal's age, like the circular ridges added year by year to the horns of the Indian buffalo.

After seeing the collections at Chamouni, Shelley added a few words about some other wild animals. He notes that there are no bears in that region, though he had heard that they were sometimes seen near Lucerne. Bears, it is known, still exist in the Jura and in some parts of the Grisons, and they occasionally make their way into the Valais. "The wolves," said Shelley, "are more powerful than the fiercest and strongest dog." "Did I tell you," he asks Peacock, "that there are troops of wolves in these mountains? In the winter they descend into the valleys, which the snow occupies six months of the year, and devour everything that they can find out of doors." He may have been thinking again of the legends of Bethgelert, or may be referring to the adventure that befell Gray and his companion, when they crossed Mont Cenis in muffs and beaver-masks, and Horace Walpole's black spaniel ran by the side of the chaise. "It was noonday, and the sun shone bright, when all of a sudden from the woodside out rushed a great wolf, caught the dog by the throat, and rushed up the hill with him in its mouth. This was done in a quarter of a minute: we all saw it, and yet the servants had not time to draw their pistols or to do anything to save the dog."

Two roads led from the village towards Chamouni. One was a mere track from the inn at Servoz to the works which the Mining Company had left standing at Foully. The other was the Route des Montées, with easier grades and more convenient in every way, though some of the earlier tourists had described it as the steepest and roughest road that ever was seen. Such as it was, Shelley determined to use this road, which had been widened and improved a short time before, so that the mules no longer jammed their riders against the cliff, and there was even room for a little light carriage to pass along. We may take from "Frankenstein" a description of what they saw after leaving the deserted lead-and-copper mine at the foot of Mont Vandagne. "Still as I ascended higher, the Valley of Servoz assumed a more magnificent and astonishing character: ruined castles hanging on the precipices and piny mountains, the impetuous Arve, and cottages here and there peeping forth from among the trees, formed a scene of singular beauty." There is a reference here to the "haunted ruin" of the Château de St. Michel, about half a league from Servoz, as to which the peasants told many wild stories of buried treasure, and fiends, and sorcerers. About a mile farther the track descends abruptly to the Pont Pélissier, which spanned the Arve and its ravine. The structure was of wood, the original stone bridge having been carried away in a flood: there was always a danger from the river, or those torrents of mud and powdered rocks from the side-valleys which the natives call the "*Nant Sauvage*," or the bursting of the pent-up waters of a glacier, such as came down the Bonnant, not long ago, to overwhelm the Baths of St. Gervais. Standing on this bridge, Shelley could look into the transverse ravine which leads straight up to Chamouni. "Mont Blanc was before us," he writes, "but it was covered with cloud; its base, furrowed with dreadful gaps, was seen above." Between the driving clouds they saw the white shapes of the Dôme and the Aiguille du Midi. If we may quote Mrs. Shelley once more, the scene was made sublime by the mighty Alps; "their white and shining pyramids and domes towered above all as belonging to another earth, the habitation of another set of beings." In the ravine above the bridge the vegetation suffers a change. The trees are of a sable rusty hue, and are huddled in a sunless crowd, though for an instant one may see the dazzling snow through a gap in the frondage. The ravine is black in its depth below, "so deep that the very roaring of the untameable Arve cannot be heard above." The Valley of Chamouni appears as one crosses the stony ridge. "The snowy mountains are its immediate boundaries. "I saw no more ruined castles," says Frankenstein: "immense glaciers approached the road: I heard the rumbling thunder of an avalanche, and marked the smoke of its passage." That avalanche has appeared in many descriptions of the scene. Shelley tells us how he felt that there was something earthly in the sound, and how they watched the whirling cloud and heard at intervals "the bursting of its fall." At one point it displaced the dark torrent that bursts from the Glacier of Taconnay, and presently they saw the "tawny-coloured waters" spread out across the ravine that formed their bed:

> Hark, the rushing snow,
> The sun-awakened avalanche! whose mass,
> Thrice sifted by the storm, had gathered there
> Flake after flake.

The first stream to cross their path was the Nant de Nayin, rolling in its channel a mixed *débris* of slate and quartz. The roofs of the well-built houses at Ouches are supplied by the vertical strata of slate in the neighbouring mountain. The muddy stream of the Gria, just outside the village, is the most dangerous of all. It comes from a small glacier of the same name, which hangs over a bed of gypsum, which is called "Gria" in the local dialect. M. Bourrit has left a vivid account of his escape when he was trying to pass the stepping-stones, and a mass of mud and water, rolling rocks and trees before it, came roaring down in a moment, "like lava from a volcano." Just beyond the Gria is the ravine of the Taconnay, where they saw the avalanche, and it was not long before they crossed a wooden bridge over the stream fed by the Glacier des Bossons. The glacier at that time was much lower on the hillside than it is at present. It had advanced about three hundred feet even during the twelvemonth that preceded Shelley's visit. "We saw this glacier, which comes close to the fertile plain, as we passed: its surface was broken into a thousand unaccountable figures; conical and pyramidical crystallisations more than fifty feet high rise from its surface, and precipices of ice of dazzling splendour overhang the woods and meadows of the vale." Two days afterwards Shelley visited the ice-fall again with his guide, of whom he says, "he is the only tolerable person that I have seen in this country." This was "Ducrée," or "Ducroz" as he would be called in the *patois*, who had apparently conducted the party all the way from St. Martin. The verge of the glacier presented a most vivid picture of desolation. The pines were overthrown and shattered at its base: the meadows perished under the accumulated sand and stones: "no one dares to approach it," says the Poet, "for the enormous pinnacles of ice, which perpetually fall, are perpetually reproduced."

PONT STE MARIE

> There many a precipice
> Frost and the sun in scorn of mortal power
> Have piled dome, pyramid, and pinnacle,
> A city of Death, distinct with many a tower
> And wall impregnable of gleaming ice:
> Yet not a city, but a flood of ruin,
> Is there, that from the boundaries of the sky
> Rolls its perpetual stream.

On arriving at "Le Prieuré," the principal village in the district, the guide took the visitors to the expensive Hôtel de Londres, then kept by M. Tairraz, assisted by his sons Jean-Pierre, Michel, and Victor; they were all experienced guides, and the innkeeper himself is stated by Mr. Coolidge to have done much towards making the mule-path up to the Montanvert. The "Angleterre," originally founded by Madame Couteran, had enjoyed the best reputation among the citizens of Geneva ever since the days of De Saussure; but we are told that her son failed to propitiate the guides of St. Martin and Sallanches, who in revenge took all their clients to the "Londres." These two inns were afterwards united under one management. M. Bourrit, describing the place about 1785, pays a high tribute of praise to the original "Angleterre"; but he says that two other *auberges* had been built, the one near the entrance of the village, belonging to M. Tairraz, and the other at the further end of the street. The history of the third inn is not quite clear. Some take it to have been connected with the "Union," kept by MM. Charles and Simond; but this house was not built until 1817, and was situated near the entrance of the village. It may be observed, however, that Sir Frederick Eden stated in his diary for 1791 that on proceeding to Chamouni in that year he found "an excellent inn, called Les Balances."

As soon as any party of travellers was reported as having arrived at their inn, they were at once assailed by guides seeking engagements, and vendors of curiosities with plants and minerals for sale, and the only hope of escape lay in promising to go as soon as possible to Paccard's Museum and the collections of Joseph Cartier and David Payot. All these men, we are assured, were persons of intelligence and even of some culture in their various ways; and Paccard, who had been one of De Saussure's guides, was specially praised as being "wise, well-instructed, and trustworthy." But Shelley appears to have been intensely irritated either by the fine appearance of the hotel, or by the pertinacity of the peasants in pressing their wares, and he includes them all, from Paccard downwards, in one sweeping blast of condemnation: "There is a cabinet of *Histoire Naturelle*, the proprietor of which is the very vilest specimen of that vile species of quack that, together with the whole army of *aubergistes* and guides, and the entire mass of the population, subsists on the weakness and credulity of travellers as leeches subsist on the sick." It would have been more entertaining if he had made acquaintance with the tribes of Couttet and Carrier and Tournier, and enquired after old Lambard, surnamed "le Grande-Jorasse," and Marie Paradis, then "Marie Frasseron *dite* Mont-Blanc," who had made the great ascent in 1809 with the Balmats and two of the young men of the Hôtel de Londres. He may even have seen the heroine, as she owned a little cottage on the mountainside, where travellers could buy souvenirs. When the great Dumas came over the Tête-Noire, after partaking of a *biftek d'Ours* at Martigny, his first thought was to send an invitation to " M. Jacques Balmat, *dit* Mont-Blanc," whom he celebrated in his "Travels" as the Christopher Columbus of Chamouni. He wanted to learn at first hand the story of 1786, when Balmat and Dr. Paccard had ascended Mont Blanc as the pioneers of De Saussure. The gray old "mountain-wolf," they say, took a long draught, and smacked his lips and blinked his eyes, and told them how he had got to the top alone, the Doctor being snow-blind and frost-bitten; "he had reached a point where no man, or eagle, or chamois, had been before; he was the King of the Mountain, the statue on the monstrous pedestal"; and all his subjects in the village below saw him drag up the Doctor, crippled as he was, to make the conquest complete. Pierre Payot, the only other guest, took Dumas next day to the Mer de Glace, and showed him the Fountain of Caillet, which, in Payot's opinion, was "immortalised" as the resort of the unfortunate shepherdess in Florian's pastoral of "Claudine."

Shelley and the ladies rode up beyond the fountain on their first expedition, but were turned back by the rain before they were much more than half-way to the ice-field. The weather had broken soon after the start, and they all returned wet through. The incident appears in "Frankenstein," with additions filled in after a later and more successful ascent. "I looked on the valley beneath: vast mists were rising from the rivers which ran through it, while rain poured from the dark sky, and added to the melancholy impression I received from the objects around me." We are told that the whole scene was "terrifically desolate," and that in a thousand spots the broken and fallen trees showed the track of the winter avalanches. The difficulties of the road are well known. It is like walking "on a steep slate-roof" two thousand feet high: at every *mauvais pas* there is a chance of rolling down to the Arveiron brawling below; there are snow-slopes and falling stones, and at one place in particular there is actual danger of being struck by fragments from a range of disintegrated rocks. "Our guides," said Shelley, " desired us to pass quickly": and only a few years before, it had been the practice to forbid talking, for fear of producing "concussion of air" sufficient to cause an accident. De Saussure, according to M. Leschevin, used to fire a pistol on reaching this point, and the discharge was always followed in a short time by a fall of loose blocks. The Hut or Cabin of Montanvert was set up under the personal superintendence of M. Bourrit. When De Saussure first began his explorations there had been nothing but a kind of cave, made by propping up a few stones under the granite boulder known after the visit of Pococke and Windham as the "Pierre des Anglais." The rough "Château de Montanvert," as some of the guides used to call it, was abandoned in favour of a cabin set up about 1779 by Mr. Charles Blair. Coxe described "Blair's cabin" in the "Travels in Switzerland" as a small but commodious wooden house; and Mr. Coolidge tells us that this hut was visited by Goethe as early as the 5th of November 1779, when he was passing through Switzerland for the second time, in company with the Grand Duke of Weimar. M. Leschevin, however, is positive that

Blair built a stone cabin in 1781, which had proved to be a great comfort to travellers, and was still standing when he published his book in 1812. On consulting the manuscript account of Sir Frederick Eden's tour in 1790 we read: "On the top of Montanvert we found a hut built of stone, called Blair's Cabin, having been erected by Charles Blair, from which we descended a little and mounted the Sea of Ice, of which I cannot give you a better idea than by comparing it to a stormy sea suddenly frozen." The hut visited by Shelley had been planned as early as 1793, but was not actually built till two years afterwards; the expenses being generously borne by M. Félix Desportes, then acting as French Resident at Geneva. M. Leschevin has described the mischievous destruction of the fittings and furniture of this "*Temple de la Nature*," as it was named from Bourrit's inscription above the door. It remained for some years, according to Mr. Coolidge, in a very pitiable state; but it was put into good order again by the Senator Le Doulcet Pontecoulant in the year 1803, and thenceforth remained in charge of M. Couteran, of the Hôtel d'Angleterre at Chamouni. In 1840 a new wing was built by the Commune of Chamouni, which was replaced in 1879 by the existing establishment.

Shelley has given us a fine picture of the Aiguille

du Dru and its three companions. The summits of the mountains, he said, are "sharp and naked pinnacles," too steep for the snows to rest: "lines of dazzling ice occupy here and there the perpendicular rifts, and shine through the driving vapours with inexpressible brilliance." Mrs. Shelley borrowed some of his phrases for her romance, and spoke of the mountains dependent on the River of Ice, with their "aërial summits" hanging over its recesses, and their "icy and glittering peaks" that shone in the sunlight above the clouds. We are tempted to add a reference to a story more suited, one would think, to Munchausen than to the veracious journals of Dr. Moore. While contemplating the Valley of Ice and the Needles, he remarks, one of the company observed that there must be a fine view from the peaks extending over the Valais and all the way to Mount Jura. "This excited the ambition of the Duke of Hamilton; he sprang up and made toward the Aiguille du Dru, the highest of the four Needles; though he bounded over the ice with the elasticity of a young chamois, it was a considerable time before he could arrive at its foot, for people are greatly deceived as to distances in those snowy regions." "Should he get near the top," cried another, "he will swear we have seen nothing; but I'll try to mount as high as he can." So saying, he sprang after him.

In a short time we saw them both scrambling up the rock. The Duke had gained a considerable height, when **he was** suddenly stopped by a part of the rock **which was** perfectly impracticable, for his impetuosity had prevented him from choosing the easiest way. The rivals took a little time "to breathe and cool," **and** finally decided that the exploit was not worth their while, since the honours of victory would be divided. But this was in the days when an ordinary traveller's tale was apt to be quenched by the remark: "Dear sir, that's **pretty well**; but take my word for it, 'tis nothing to the Glaciers of Savoy!"

The vale itself, says Shelley, is filled with a mass of undulating ice: its appearance was "as if frost had suddenly bound up the waves and whirlpools of a mighty torrent." "The waves," he continues, "are elevated about twelve or fourteen feet from the surface of the mass, which is intersected by long gaps of unfathomable depth, the ice of whose sides is more **beautifully azure** than the sky. In these regions everything changes and is in motion; this vast mass of ice has one general progress which ceases neither day nor night; it breaks and bursts for ever; some undulations sink while others rise: it is never the same." We are reminded of the fantastic theories of a time **long** preceding De Saussure. It looks as if Shelley **were** referring to the accounts published in

the *Mercure Suisse* for 1743, soon after Pococke's return from Chamouni. A few sentences may be taken from some of these letters as they appear in an unpublished English version of Gruner now in the writer's possession: "The surface of the ice is rent in places. The clefts are of various dimensions, the largest being about twenty feet long, and from four to five feet in breadth." It will be remembered that these observations are very inaccurate, especially with regard to the *crevasses* and to the periods after which there has been a recovery of the bodies of persons who have perished in them. "These rents are generally in the weakest part of the ice in the scoop of the waves, and run as they do, awry and sideways. We judged of the thickness of the ice by these clefts, and found it apparently from five to six feet, but in other places it may be from fifty to sixty feet. These rents always take place with an explosion like thunder. The water under the ice appears through these clefts. Our guides pushed a stick into the water, and let it go, but it rose again of itself, from which it may be inferred that the waters touched the ceiling of the ice. If a person has the misfortune to fall into one of these chasms, which sometimes happens to the crystal-diggers, the body is found within a few days after, thrown out upon the ice, quite fresh, especially when there has been some rain, or the weather has grown milder. The reason of the bodies being thrown up again in this manner seems to be that on an increase of water the fluid, finding no vent below, seeks its way out above through these rents, and pushes whatever comes in its way before it. The inhabitants insist that the glaciers have a regular increase and decrease, and probably this is the case; but it is the prevailing opinion that they rather increase than decrease." When Marie Couttet escaped from his terrible fall into the *crevasse* on the *Grand Plateau*, the bodies of the guides who were lost were not recovered for more than forty years afterwards. Even the scientific M. de la Condamine described the Mer de Glace as being alternately melted and congealed, and spoke of "the subterranean torrent which supports this enormous mass, and changes its appearance as well as its level from day to day."

Shelley writes very positively on the subject of glacier-motion. "De Saussure the naturalist" had maintained that there were periods of advance and retreat: "The people of the country hold an opinion entirely different, but as I judge more probable." M. Bourrit and some of his friends appealed to experience. The old people at Chamouni used to say that they remembered the time when the glaciers were very much smaller, and when they could walk behind the Mer de Glace by passages "now choked with hills of snow not fifty years old." This may have been merely a reflection of a story told by the Greffier of Chamouni, who said that the Mer de Glace covered a road by which the villagers used to go to the Court at Courmayeur four centuries ago. M. Patience, of the Great House at Courmayeur, was positive that several of the glaciers had left their old beds since he first came up to hunt *bouquetins* on Mont Mallet. M. Bourrit noticed a great increase in the ice-fields on the Talèfre and at the back of the Aiguilles de Charmoz, where within his recollection there had been a Golconda for the crystal-men and good store of *génipi*, or yarrow, of which the *bouquetins* and chamois were so fond. Shelley was alarmed at the prospect of a return of the Glacial Age. He would not discuss the gloomy theory of Buffon, that the polar ice-caps might creep on till they joined the central snow-fields; but if the snow, he argues, is continually heaped up above, while the ice remains unmelted in the transient and variable summers below, surely the glaciers will be augmented, "at least until they overwhelm this vale." Such theories, said Dr. Moore, are well-fabricated and goodly to behold; and nothing is more vexatious than to see them upset by the dash of a pen, as a house falls down in the pantomime at a slap from the Harlequin's wand. If the glaciers go on increasing *ad infinitum*, the great globe will become "an appendage of Mont Blanc": the authors of the theory must regret that they were sent into the world so soon; "because, if their birth had been delayed nine or ten thousand years, they would have seen the glaciers in much greater glory, Mont Blanc being but a Lilliputian at present in comparison to what it will be then."

Shelley bids his friend Peacock, who asserted "the supremacy of Ahriman," to imagine the King of Evil enthroned among those desolate snows: he sits in the palaces of Death and Frost, and casts around us his first essays of usurpation, "avalanches, torrents, rocks, and thunders, and above all, these deadly glaciers, at once the proof and symbol of his reign." We ought, perhaps, to observe how Byron dealt with the same idea in "Manfred," which was finished in the February of 1817. The three Fates or Destinies appear on the summit of the Jungfrau on their way to the "Hall of Arimanes," and the description of their place of meeting is evidently taken from Shelley's account of the Mer de Glace:

> O'er the savage sea,
> The glassy ocean of the mountain-ice,
> We skim its rugged breakers, which put on
> The aspect of a tumbling tempest's foam,
> Frozen in a moment, a dead whirlpool's image,

> And this most steep fantastic pinnacle,
> The fretwork of some earthquake.

In another part of his sketch Shelley has employed a curious classical metaphor which bears some analogy to the speech of Mother Earth in the "Prometheus Unbound":

> Thy touch runs down
> Even to the adamantine central gloom
> Along these marble nerves : 'tis life, 'tis joy,
> And through my withered old and icy frame
> The warmth of an immortal youth shoots down
> Circling.

Shelley is speaking of the incessant noise that fills the air in the neighbourhood of the Mer de Glace. The echo from the rocks, and the din of the ice and snow, which fall from the cliffs or roll from the summits, never seem to pause for a moment. He refers, in a somewhat inaccurate way, to the belief of the ancient Stoics, that the Cosmos and its Maker formed the perfect Unity. But when he compares Mont Blanc to the God of the Stoics we should remember that it was only our Earth, and not the whole Universe, which they regarded as a Leviathan, breathing in storms and spouting in tides, and warmed with volcanic fire. "One would think," he says, "that Mont Blanc was a vast animal, and that the frozen blood for ever circulated through his stony veins."

They dined on the grassy sward near the hut, "surrounded by this scene," in a clear and piercing air, and returned by the way that they came, not caring to follow the steep descent that would have brought them to the source of the Arveiron again.

Before returning to Montalègre, Shelley seems to have somewhat relented towards the "*Marchands Naturalistes.*" "We have bought," he says, "some specimens of minerals and plants, and two or three crystal seals at Mont Blanc, to preserve the remembrance of having approached it." David Payot was the principal cutter of these seals, which were generally made of the spar from Dauphiné, and as he lived at Praz d'Avaz, or the "Lower Meadows," we may suppose that Shelley made this part of his purchase on returning from the Glacier des Bossons. The best general collection was that which belonged to Carrier, whose catalogue of "sixty-six specimens from Chamouni" may be seen in the *Journal des Mines* for 1809. A great part of his specimens came from the Montanvert and the Aiguilles behind it, where the guides had found many "*fours à cristaux*" in the quartz. One of the best filled had been discovered close to the Fountain of Caillet. The bed of the Arveiron was rich in jasper and porphyry, auriferous sand, and the potstone and serpentine out of which letter-weights and lamps were carved. But the interest of the collection was somewhat spoiled by the intrusion of such foreign visitors as the bits from the Simplon and the St. Gothard, the Valais and the Val d'Aosta, and the inevitable painted onyx from the manufactories of Oberstein on the Rhine. The plants arranged for the *Hortus Siccus* included all the varieties from the "Jardin" high up on the Mer de Glace and the oasis of the Talèfre, such as the gentians, and the creeping azaleas, and rhododendrons that haunt the margin of the ice. "The most interesting of my purchases," writes Shelley, "is a large collection of all the seeds of rare Alpine plants, with their names written upon the outside of the papers that contain them: these I mean to colonise in my garden in England, and to permit you to make what choice you please from them." We do not suppose that many of them emerged into the light among the rough hillocks of the garden at Marlow. He ends with an affectionate thought of Wordsworth's two odes to his favourite flower. "They are companions," he wrote, "which the Celandine, the classic Celandine, need not despise; they are as wild and more daring than he, and will tell him tales of things even as touching and sublime as the gaze of a Vernal Poet":

Ere a leaf is on a bush
In the time before the thrush
Has a thought about her nest,
Thou wilt come with half a call,
Like a careless prodigal:
Telling tales about the sun,
When we've little warmth or none.

  * * * * * *

Blithe of heart from week to week
Thou dost play at hide-and-seek:
While the patient primrose sits
 Like a beggar in the cold,
Thou, a flower of wiser wits,
 Slipst into thy sheltering hold:
Bright as any of the train,
When ye all are out again!

A LIST OF THE PRINCIPAL WORKS TO WHICH REFERENCE HAS BEEN MADE

1. ANNALES et Journal des Mines. (Journal. Nos. 4, 5, 7, 10, 26, &c. 1794–1809). Paris, 1794–1870.
2. BOURRIT, Marc-Théodore. Nouvelle description générale et particulière des Glacières, Vallées de Glace, et Glaciers, qui forment la grande chaîne des Alpes de Savoye, de Suisse, et d'Italie. Par M. Bourrit, Chantre de l'Eglise Cathédrale de Genève, et Pensionnaire du Roi de France. Genève, 1787. 8vo. 3 vols.
3. BYRON, George Gordon Noel, Lord Byron. The Prisoner of Chillon, and other Poems. London, J. Murray. 1816. 8vo.
4. —— Childe Harold's Pilgrimage. Canto the Third. London, J. Murray. 1816. 8vo.
5. —— Manfred, a Dramatic Poem. London, J. Murray. 1817. 8vo.
6. —— Lord Byron's Poetical Works. London, J. Murray. 1837. 8vo.
7. COOLIDGE, W. A. B. Swiss Travel and Swiss Guide-books. London, Longmans. 1889. 8vo.
8. DUMAS, Alexandre. Impressions de Voyage. Suisse. Paris, Lévy. 1851. 12mo, 3 vols.
9. ECKERMANN, Johann Peter. Gespräche mit Goethe in den letzen Jahren seines Lebens. Leipzig. 1836–48. 8vo. 3 vols.
10. —— Conversations of Goethe with Eckerman and Sorel. Translated from the German by John Oxenford. London, Bell. 1874. 8vo.

11. EDEN, Frederick Morton. Abstract of a Tour performed in 1790 by Sir Fred. M. Eden and Charles J. Harford. (MS. unpublished.)
12. GIBBON, Edward. The History of the Decline and Fall of the Roman Empire. With an Introductory Memoir of the Author by William Youngman. London, 1837. 8vo.
13. GRAY, Thomas. The Poems of Mr. Gray. To which are prefixed Memoirs of his Life and Writings. By W. Mason. London, 1775. 4to.
14. GRUNER, Gottlieb Sigmund. Die Eisgebirge des Schweizerlandes. Bern, 1760. 8vo.
15. —— Histoire Naturelle des Glacières de la Suisse. Traduite par M. de Kéralio. Paris, 1770. 4to.
16. —— The Icy Mountains of Swisserland, described by the Sieur Gottlieb Sigmund Gruner, Advocate to the Two-Hundreds in the Republick of Bern, translated from the German. (MS. unpublished, *s.a.*) Fol. 3 vols.
17. HUGO, Victor. En Voyage : Alpes et Pyrénées. Paris, 1890. 8vo.
18. KOCH, Frédéric. Mémoires pour servir à l'histoire de la Campagne de 1814. Paris, 1819. 8vo. 2 vols.
19. LA CONDAMINE, Charles-Marie de. Journal d'un Voyage en Italie (Mémoires presentées à l'Académie). Paris, 1762. 4to.
20. —— Journal of a Tour to Italy, containing amongst many other interesting and curious particulars Remarks on the Mountains and Ice-valleys of Swisserland, &c. London, 1763. 12mo.
21. LESCHEVIN, Philippe-Xavier. Voyage à Genève et dans la Vallée de Chamouni en Savoie. Paris et Genève, 1812. 12mo.
22. MEDWIN, Thomas. The Shelley Papers. Memoir of Percy Bysshe Shelley. By T. Medwin, Esq. And Original Poems by Percy Bysshe Shelley. Now first collected. London, 1833. 8vo.
23. MERCURE SUISSE. Relations des premiers voyages faits aux Glaciers de la Vallée de Chamouni en 1742. Mai et Juin, 1742. Neufchâtel, 1743. Fol.

WORKS CITED

24. MONTAGUE, Mary Wortley, Lady. Letters of the Right Honourable Lady M——y W——y M——e; written during her Travels in Europe, Asia and Africa, to persons of distinction, men of letters, &c., in different parts of Europe. London, 1778. 8vo. 2 vols.
25. MOORE, John. A View of Society and Manners in France, Switzerland, and Germany, with Anecdotes relating to some Eminent Characters. By John Moore, M.D. Dublin, 1780. 12mo. 2 vols.
26. MOORE, Thomas. Lord Byron's Life, Letters, and Journals. Edited by Thomas Moore. London, 1830. 4to. 2 vols.
27. PACCARD, Michel. Premier voyage fait à la cime de la plus haute montagne du continent; par M. le Docteur Paccard. (Lausanne.) 1786. 8vo.
28. PLANTIN, Johann Baptist. Helvetia Antiqua et Nova. Bern, 1656. 8vo.
29. RAY, John. Observations topographical, moral, and physiological, made in a journey through part of the Low Countries, Germany, Italy, and France: with a Catalogue of Plants, not native of England, found spontaneously growing in those parts, and their virtues, &c. London, Martyn. 1673. 8vo.
30. SAUSSURE, Horace-Bénédict de. Voyages dans les Alpes, précédés d'un Essai sur l' histoire naturelle des Environs de Genève. Neufchâtel, 1779–86–96. 4to. 4 vols.
31. SHELLEY, Percy Bysshe. Alastor, or the Spirit of Solitude, and other Poems. London, Baldwin, 1816. 8vo.
32. —— The Revolt of Islam, a Poem in Twelve Cantos. London, Ollier, 1818. 8vo.
33. —— Prometheus Unbound. A Lyrical Drama in four Acts, with other Poems. London, Ollier, 1820. 8vo.
34. —— The Complete Poetical Works of Percy Bysshe Shelley. The text carefully revised, with notes and a memoir, by William Michael Rossetti. London, 1881. 8vo. 3 vols.
35. SHELLEY, Mary Wollstonecraft. Frankenstein, or the Modern Prometheus. London, Lackington, 1817. 8vo.
36. —— Frankenstein, or the Modern Prometheus. London, Colburn, 1831. 8vo.

37. SHELLEY, Mary Wollstonecraft. Shelley Memorials. Edited by **Lady Shelley**. London, 1859. 8vo.
38. TRELAWNY, **Edward** John. Recollections of the Last Days of Shelley and Byron. London, 1858. 8vo.
39. WOLLSTONECRAFT, Mary. Letters written during a short residence in Sweden, Norway, and Denmark. London, 1796. **8vo.**
40. WORDSWORTH, **William. Poems** by W. Wordsworth, author of Lyrical Ballads. London, 1807. 12mo. **2 vols.**
41. ——— The Excursion, being a portion of The Recluse, **a** Poem. London, 1814. 4to.
42. ——— Memorials of a Tour on the Continent, 1820. London, 1822. 8vo.
43. ——— The Poetical **Works** of William Wordsworth. A new **edition.** London, 1836. 8vo. **6 vols.**
44. ——— The Recluse, by **William** Wordsworth. London, Macmillan, 1888. 12mo.

(EXTRACTS.)

HISTORY OF A SIX WEEKS' TOUR

THROUGH A PART OF FRANCE, SWITZERLAND,

GERMANY, AND HOLLAND

WITH LETTERS DESCRIPTIVE OF A SAIL ROUND THE

LAKE OF GENEVA, AND OF THE GLACIERS

OF CHAMOUNI

LONDON: 1817

EXTRACTS FROM

Journal, 1814.
Letters, 1816.

A SIX WEEKS' TOUR

I. PREFACE

NOTHING can be more unpresuming than this little volume. It contains the account of some desultory visits by a party of young people to scenes which are now so familiar to our countrymen that few facts relating to them can be expected to have escaped the many more experienced and exact observers who have sent their journals to the press. In fact, they have done little else than arrange the few materials which an imperfect journal and two or three letters to their friends in England afforded. They regret, since their little history is to be offered to the public, that these materials were not more copious and complete. This is a just topic of censure to those who are less inclined to be amused than to condemn. Those whose youth has been past as theirs (with what success it imports not) in pursuing, like the swallow, the inconstant summer of delight and beauty which invests this visible world, will perhaps find some entertainment in following the author with her husband and sister, on foot through part of France and Switzerland, and in sailing with her down the castled Rhine, through scenes beautiful in themselves, but which, since she visited them, a great poet has clothed with the freshness of a diviner nature. They will be interested to hear of one who has visited Meillerie, and Clarens, and Chillon, and Vevey, classic ground peopled with tender and glorious imaginations of the present and the past.

They have perhaps never talked with one who has beheld in the enthusiasm of youth the glaciers, and the lakes, and the forests, and the fountains of the mighty Alps. Such will perhaps forgive the imperfections of their narrative for the sympathy which the adventures and feelings which it recounts, and a curiosity respecting scenes already rendered interesting and illustrious, may excite.

The poem entitled "Mont Blanc" is written by the author of the two letters from Chamouni and Vevey. It was composed under the immediate impression of the deep and powerful feelings excited by the objects which it attempts to describe; and, as an undisciplined overflowing of the soul, rests its claim to approbation on an attempt to imitate the untameable wildness and inaccessible solemnity from which those feelings sprang.

II. INTRODUCTION

It is now nearly three years since this journey took place, and the journal I then kept was not very copious; but I have so often talked over the incidents that befell us, and attempted to describe the scenery through which we passed, that I think few occurrences of any interest will be omitted.

We left London July 28th, 1814, on a hotter day than has been known in this climate for many years. I am not a good traveller, and this heat agreed very ill with me, till on arriving at Dover I was refreshed by a sea-bath. As we very much wished to cross the Channel with all possible speed, we would not wait for the Packet of the following day, (it being then about four in the afternoon,) but hiring a small boat, resolved to make the passage the same evening, the seamen promising us a voyage of two hours.

The evening was most beautiful; there was but little wind, and the sails flapped in the flagging breeze: the moon rose, and night came on, and with the night a slow heavy swell and a fresh breeze, which soon produced a sea so violent as to toss the boat very much. I was dreadfully sea-sick, and as is usually my custom when thus affected, I slept during the greater part of the night, awaking only from time to time to ask where we were, and to receive the dismal answer each time, "Not quite half-way."

The wind was violent and contrary; if we could not reach Calais, the sailors proposed making for Boulogne. They promised only two hours' sail from shore, yet hour after hour passed and we were still far distant, when the moon sunk in the red and stormy horizon, and the fast-flashing lightning became pale in the breaking day.

We were proceeding slowly against the wind, when suddenly a thunder-squall struck the sail, and the waves rushed into the boat: even the sailors acknowledged that our situation was perilous; but they succeeded in reefing the sail; the wind was now changed, and we drove before the gale directly to Calais. As we entered the harbour I awoke from a comfortless sleep, and saw the sun rise, broad, red, and cloudless, over the pier.

III. FRANCE.

EXHAUSTED with sickness and fatigue, I walked over the sands with my companions to the hotel. I heard for the first time the confused buzz of voices speaking a different language from that to which I had been accustomed, and saw a costume very unlike that worn on the opposite side of the Channel; the women with high caps and short jackets; the men with earrings; ladies walking about with high bonnets or *coiffures* lodged on the top of the head, the hair dragged up underneath, without any stray curls to decorate the temples or cheeks. There is, however, something very pleasing in the manners and appearance of the people of Calais, that prepossesses you in their favour. A national reflection might occur, that when Edward III. took Calais, he turned out the old inhabitants, and peopled it almost entirely with our own countrymen; but unfortunately the manners are not English.

We remained during that day and the greater part of the next at Calais: we had been obliged to leave our boxes the night before at the English Customhouse, and it was arranged that they should go by the Packet of the following day, which detained by contrary wind did not arrive until night. S. and I walked among the fortifications on the outside of the town; they consisted of fields where the hay was making. The aspect of the country was rural and pleasant.

On the 30th of July, about three in the afternoon, we left Calais in a cabriolet drawn by three horses. To persons who had never before seen anything but a spruce English chaise and postboy, there was something irresistibly ludicrous in our equipage. A cabriolet is shaped somewhat like a post-chaise, except that it has only two wheels, and consequently there are no doors at the sides; the front is let down to admit the passengers. The three horses were placed abreast, the tallest in the middle, who was rendered more formidable by the addition of an unintelligible article of harness, resembling a pair of wooden wings fastened to his shoulders; the harnesses were of rope; and the postillion, a queer upright little fellow with a long pigtail, *craquée'd* his whip and clattered on, while an old forlorn shepherd with a cocked hat gazed on us as we passed.

The roads are excellent, but the heat was intense, and I suffered greatly from it. We slept at Boulogne the first night, where there was an ugly but remarkably good-tempered *Femme de chambre*.

We had ordered horses to be ready during the night, but we were too fatigued to make use of them. The man insisted on being paid for the whole post. "*Ah! madame*," said the *Femme de chambre*, "*Pensez-y! C'est pour dédommager les pauvres chevaux d'avoir perdu leur douce sommeil.*"

The first appearance that struck our English eyes was the want of inclosures; but the fields were flourishing with a plentiful harvest. We observed no vines on this side Paris.

The weather still continued very hot, and travelling produced a very bad effect upon my health; my companions were induced by this circumstance to hasten the journey as much as possible; and accordingly we did not rest the following night, and the next day, about two, arrived in Paris.

In this city there are no hotels where you can reside as long or as short a time as you please, and we were obliged to engage apartments at an hotel for a week. They were dear, and not very pleasant. As usual in France, the principal apartment was a bedchamber; there was another closet with a bed, and an antechamber which we used as a sitting-room.

The heat of the weather was excessive, so that we were unable to walk except in the afternoon. On the first evening we walked to the gardens of the Tuileries; they are formal, in the French fashion, the trees cut into shapes, and without grass. I think the Boulevards infinitely more pleasant. This street nearly surrounds Paris, and is eight miles in extent; it is very wide, and planted on either side with trees. At one end is a superb cascade, which refreshes the senses by its continual splashing: near this stands the Gate of St. Denis, a beautiful piece of sculpture. I do not know how it may at present be disfigured by the Gothic barbarism of the conquerors of France, who were not contented with retaking the spoils of Napoleon, but with impotent malice destroyed the monuments of their own defeat. When I saw this Gate it was in its splendour, and made you imagine that the days of Roman greatness were transported to Paris.

After remaining a week in Paris, we received a small remittance that set us free from a kind of imprisonment there which we found very irksome. But how should we proceed? After talking over and rejecting many plans, we fixed on one, eccentric enough, but which from its romance was very pleasing to us. In England we could not have put it in execution without sustaining continual insult and impertinence: the French are far more tolerant of the vagaries of their neighbours. We resolved to walk through France; but as I was too weak for any considerable distance, and my sister could not be supposed to be able to walk as far as S. each day, we determined to purchase an ass, to carry our portmanteau and one of us by turns.

Early therefore on Monday, August 8, S. and C. went to the ass-market and purchased an ass, and the rest of the day, until four in the afternoon, was spent in making preparations for our departure, during which Madame l'Hôte paid us a visit, and attempted to dissuade us from our design. She represented to us

Porte St Denis.

that a large army had been recently disbanded, that the soldiers and officers wandered idle about the country, and that "*Les dames seraient certainement enlevées.*" But we were proof against her arguments, and packing up a few necessaries, leaving the rest to go by the diligence, we departed in a *fiacre* from the door of the hotel, our little ass following.

We dismissed the coach at the barrier. It was dusk, and the ass seemed totally unable to bear one of us, appearing to sink under the portmanteau, although it was small and light. We were, however, merry enough, and thought the leagues short. We arrived at Charenton about ten.

Charenton is prettily situated in a valley through which the Seine flows, winding among banks variegated with trees. On looking at this scene, C. exclaimed, "Oh! this is beautiful enough; let us live here." This was her exclamation on every new scene, and as each surpassed the one before, she cried, "I am glad we did not stay at Charenton, but let us live here."

Finding our ass useless, we sold it before we proceeded on our journey, and bought a mule for ten napoleons. About nine o'clock we departed. We were clad in black silk. I rode on the mule, which carried also our portmanteau; S. and C. followed, bringing a small basket of provisions. At about one we arrived at Grosbois, where under the shade of trees we ate our bread and fruit and drank our wine, thinking of Don Quixote and Sancho.

The country through which we passed was highly cultivated but uninteresting; the horizon scarcely ever extended beyond the circumference of a few fields, bright and waving with the golden harvest. We met several travellers; but our mode, although novel, did not appear to excite any curiosity or remark. This night we slept at Guignes, in the same room and beds in which Napoleon and some of his Generals had rested during the late war. The little old woman of the place was highly gratified in having this little story to tell, and spoke in warm praise of the Empress Joséphine and Marie-Louise, who had at different times passed on that road.

As we continued our route, Provins was the first place that struck us with interest. It was our stage of rest for the night; we approached it at sunset. After having gained the summit of a hill, the prospect of the town opened upon us as it lay in the valley below; a rocky hill rose abruptly on one side, on the top of which stood a ruined citadel with extensive walls and towers; lower down but beyond was the cathedral, and the whole formed a scene for painting. After having travelled for two days through a country perfectly without interest, it was a delicious relief for the eye to dwell again on some irregularities and beauty of country. Our fare at Provins was coarse, and our beds uncomfortable, but the remembrance of this prospect made us contented and happy.

We now approached scenes that reminded us of what we had nearly forgotten, that France had lately been the country in which great and extraordinary events had taken place. Nogent, a town we entered about noon the following day, had been entirely desolated by the Cossacks. Nothing could be more entire than the ruin which these barbarians had spread as they advanced; perhaps they remembered Moscow and the destruction of the Russian villages; but we were now in France, and the distress of the inhabitants, whose houses had been burned, their cattle killed, and all their wealth destroyed, has given a sting to my detestation of war, which none can feel who have not travelled through a country pillaged and wasted by this plague, which in his pride man inflicts upon his fellow.

We quitted the Great Route soon after we had left Nogent, to strike across the country to Troyes. About six in the evening we arrived at St Aubin, a lovely village embosomed in trees; but on a nearer view we found the cottages roofless, the rafters black, and the walls dilapidated ; a few inhabitants remained. We asked for milk, they had none to give ; all their cows had been taken by the Cossacks. We had still some leagues to travel that night, but we found that they were not post leagues, but the measurement of the inhabitants, and nearly double the distance. The road lay over a desert plain, and as night advanced we were often in danger of losing the track of wheels, which was our only guide. Night closed in, and we suddenly lost all trace of the road ; but a few trees, indistinctly seen, seemed to indicate the position of a village. About ten we arrived at Trois Maisons, where after a supper on milk and sour bread we retired to rest on wretched beds : but sleep is seldom denied, except to the indolent, and after the day's fatigue, although my bed was nothing more than a sheet spread upon straw, I slept soundly until the morning was considerably advanced.

S. had hurt his ankle so considerably the preceding evening, that he was obliged during the whole of the following day's journey to ride on our mule. Nothing could be more barren and wretched than the track through which we now passed ; the ground was chalky and uncovered even by grass, and where there had been any attempts made towards cultivation, the straggling ears of corn discovered more plainly the barren nature of the soil. Thousands of insects, which were of the same white colour as the road, infested our path; the sky was cloudless, and the sun darted its rays upon us, reflected back by the earth, until I nearly fainted under the heat. A village appeared at a distance, cheering us with a prospect of rest. It gave us new strength to proceed; but it was a wretched place, and afforded us but little relief. It had been once large and populous, but now the houses were roofless, and the ruins that lay scattered about, the gardens covered with the white dust of the torn cottages, the black burnt beams, and squalid looks of the inhabitants, presented in every direction the melancholy aspect of devastation. One house, a *cabaret*, alone remained; we were here offered plenty of milk, bacon, sour bread, and a few vegetables, which we were to dress for ourselves.

As we prepared our dinner the people of the village collected around us, squalid with dirt. They seemed, indeed, entirely detached from the rest of the world, and ignorant of all that was passing in it. There is much less communication between the various towns of France than in England. The use of passports may easily account for this: these people did not know that Napoleon was deposed, and when we asked why they did not rebuild their cottages, they replied that they were afraid that the Cossacks would destroy them again upon their return. Echemine (the name of this village) is in every respect the most disgusting place I ever met with.

Two leagues beyond, on the same road, we came to the village of Pavillon, so unlike Echemine that we might have fancied ourselves in another quarter of the globe; here everything denoted cleanliness and hospitality; many of the cottages were destroyed, but the inhabitants were employed in repairing them. What could occasion so great a difference?

Still our road lay over this track of uncultivated country, and our eyes were fatigued by observing nothing but a white expanse of ground, where no bramble or stunted shrub adorned its barrenness. Towards evening we reached a small plantation of vines: it appeared like one of those islands of verdure that are met with in the midst of the sands of Lybia, but the grapes were not yet ripe. S. was totally incapable of walking, and C. and I were very tired before we arrived at Troyes.

We rested here for the night, and devoted the following day to a consideration of the manner in which we should proceed. S'. sprain rendered our pedestrianism impossible. We accordingly sold our mule, and bought an open *voiture* that went on four wheels, for five napoleons, and hired a man with a mule for eight more, to convey us to Neuchâtel in six days.

The suburbs of Troyes were destroyed, and the town itself dirty and uninviting. I remained at the inn writing, while S. and C. arranged this bargain and visited the cathedral of the town; and the next morning we departed in our *voiture* for Neuchâtel. A curious instance of French vanity occurred on leaving this town. Our *Voiturier* pointed to the plain around, and mentioned that it had been the scene of a battle between the Russians and the French. "In which the Russians gained the victory?" "Ah no, Madame," replied the man, "the French are never beaten." "But how was it then," we asked, "that the Russians had entered Troyes soon after?" "Oh! after having been defeated they took a circuitous route, and thus entered the town."

Vandœuvres is a pleasant town, at which we rested during the hours of noon. We walked in the grounds of a nobleman, laid out in the English taste, and terminated in a pretty wood; it was a scene that reminded us of our native country. As we left Vandœuvres the aspect of the country suddenly changed; abrupt hills, covered with vineyards intermixed with trees, enclosed a narrow valley, the channel of the Aube. The view was interspersed by green meadows, groves of poplar and white willow, and spires of village churches which the Cossacks had yet spared. Many villages, ruined by the war, occupied the most romantic spots.

In the evening we arrived at Bar-sur-Aube, a beautiful town, placed at the opening of the vale where the hills terminate abruptly. We climbed the highest of these, but scarce had we reached the top when a mist descended upon everything, and the rain began to fall: we were wet through before we could reach our inn. It was evening, and the laden clouds made the darkness almost as deep as that of midnight; but in the West an unusually brilliant and fiery redness occupied an opening in the vapours, and added to the interest of our little expedition : the cottage lights were reflected in the tranquil river, and the dark hills behind, dimly seen, resembled vast and frowning mountains.

As we quitted Bar-sur-Aube, we at the same time bade a short farewell to hills. Passing through the towns of Chamont, Langres, (which was situated on a hill and surrounded by ancient fortifications,) Champlitte, and Gray, we travelled for nearly three days through plains, where the country gently undulated and relieved the eye from a perpetual flat, without exciting any peculiar interest. Gentle rivers, their banks ornamented by a few trees, stole through these plains, and a thousand beautiful summer insects skimmed over the streams. The third day was a day of rain, and the first that had taken place during our journey. We were soon wet through, and were glad to stop at a little inn to dry ourselves. The reception we received here was very unprepossessing; the people still kept their seats round the fire, and seemed very unwilling to make way for the dripping guests. In the afternoon, however, the weather became fine, and at about six in the evening we entered Besançon.

Hills had appeared in the distance during the whole day, and we had advanced gradually towards them, but were unprepared for the scene that broke upon us as we passed the gate of this city. On quitting the walls the road wound underneath a high precipice; on the other side the hills rose more gradually, and the green valley that intervened between them was watered by a pleasant river; before us arose an amphitheatre of hills covered with vines, but irregular and rocky. The last gate of the town was cut through the precipitous rock that arose on one side, and in that place jutted into the road.

This approach to mountain scenery filled us with delight; it was otherwise with our *Voiturier*: he came from the plains of Troyes, and these hills so utterly scared him, that he in some degree lost his reason. After winding through the valley, we began to ascend the mountains which were its boundary: we left our *voiture* and walked on, delighted with every new view that broke upon us.

When we had ascended the hills for about a mile and a half, we found our *Voiturier* at the door of a wretched inn, having taken the mule from the *voiture* and obstinately determined to remain for the night at this miserable village of Mort. We could only submit, for he was deaf to all we could urge, and to our remonstrances only replied, "*Je ne puis pas.*"

Our beds were too uncomfortable to allow a thought of sleeping in them: we could only procure one room, and our hostess gave us to understand that our *Voiturier* was to occupy the same apartment. It was of little consequence, as we had previously resolved not to enter the beds. The evening was fine, and after the rain the air was perfumed by many delicious scents. We climbed to a rocky seat on the hill that overlooked the village, where we remained until sunset. The night was passed by the kitchen fire in a wretched manner, striving to catch a few moments of sleep, which were denied to us. At three in the morning we pursued our journey.

Our road led to the summit of the hills that environ Besançon. From the top of one of these we saw the whole expanse of the valley filled with a white undulating mist, which was pierced, (like islands,) by the piny mountains. The sun had just risen, and a ray of red light lay upon the waves of this fluctuating vapour. To the West, opposite the sun, it seemed driven by the light against the rocks in immense masses of foaming cloud, until it became lost in the distance, mixing its tints with the fleecy sky.

Our *Voiturier* insisted on remaining two hours at the village of Noë, although we were unable to procure any dinner, and wished to go on to the next stage. I have already said that the hills scared his senses, and he had become disobliging, sullen, and stupid. While he waited we walked to the neighbouring wood: it was a fine forest, carpeted beautifully with moss, and in various places overhung by rocks, in whose crevices young pines had taken root and spread their branches for shade to those below; the noon heat was intense, and we were glad to shelter ourselves from it in the shady retreats of this lovely forest.

On our return to the village we found, to our extreme surprise, that the *Voiturier* had departed nearly an hour before, leaving word that he expected to meet us on the road. S.' sprain rendered him incapable of much exertion; but there was no remedy, and we proceeded on foot to Maison Neuve, an *auberge* four miles and a half distant.

At Maison Neuve the man had left word that he should proceed to Pontarlier, the frontier town of France, six leagues distant, and that if we did not arrive that night he should the next morning leave the *voiture* at an inn, and return with the mule to Troyes. We were astonished at the impudence of this message, but the boy of the inn comforted us by saying that by going on a horse by a cross road, where the *voiture* could not venture, he could easily overtake and intercept the *Voiturier*, and accordingly we dispatched him, walking slowly after. We waited at the next inn for dinner, and in about two hours the boy returned. The man promised to wait for us at an *auberge* two leagues farther on. S.' ankle had become very painful, but we could procure no conveyance, and as the sun was nearly setting we were obliged to hasten on. The evening was most beautiful, and the scenery lovely enough to beguile us of our fatigue: the horned moon hung in the light of sunset that threw a glow of unusual depth of redness over the piny mountains and the dark deep valleys they enclosed; at intervals in the woods were beautiful lawns interspersed with picturesque clumps of trees, and dark pines overshadowed our road.

In about two hours we arrived at the promised termination of our journey, but the *Voiturier* was not there: after the boy had left him, he again pursued his journey towards Pontarlier. We were enabled, however, to procure here a rude kind of cart, and in this manner arrived late at Pontarlier, where we found our conductor, who blundered out many falsehoods for excuses; and thus ended the adventures of that day.

IV. SWITZERLAND AND THE RHINE

On passing the French barrier a surprising difference may be observed between the opposite nations that inhabit either side. The Swiss cottages are much cleaner and neater, and the inhabitants exhibit the same contrast. The Swiss women wear a great deal of white linen, and their whole dress is always perfectly clean. This superior cleanliness is chiefly produced by the difference of religion: travellers in Germany remark the same contrast between the Protestant and Catholic towns, although they be but a few leagues separate.

The scenery of this day's journey was divine, exhibiting piny mountains, barren rocks, and spots of verdure surpassing imagination. After descending for nearly a league between lofty rocks, covered with pines and interspersed with green glades, where the grass is short and soft and beautifully verdant, we arrived at the village of St. Sulpice.

The mule had latterly become very lame, and the man so disobliging, that we determined to engage a horse for the remainder of the way. Our *Voiturier* had anticipated us, without in the least intimating his intention: he had determined to leave us at this village and taken measures to that effect. The man we now engaged was a Swiss, a cottager of the better class, who was proud of his mountains and his country. Pointing to the glades that were interspersed among the woods, he informed us that they were very beautiful and were excellent pasture; that the cows thrived there, and consequently produced excellent milk, from which the best cheese and butter in the world were made.

The mountains after St. Sulpice became loftier and more beautiful. We passed through a narrow valley between two ranges of mountains, clothed with forests, at the bottom of which flowed a river from whose narrow bed on either side the boundaries of the vale arose precipitously. The road lay about half-way up the mountain, which formed one of the sides, and we saw the overhanging rocks above us,

and below enormous pines, and the river, not to be perceived but from its reflection of the light of heaven far beneath. The mountains of this beautiful ravine are so little asunder that in time of war with France an iron chain is thrown across it. Two leagues from Neuchâtel we saw the Alps: range after range of black mountains are seen extending one before the other, and far behind all, towering above every feature of the scene, the snowy Alps. They were an hundred miles distant, but reach so high in the heavens that they look like those accumulated clouds of dazzling white that arrange themselves on the horizon during summer. Their immensity staggers the imagination, and so far surpasses all conception that it requires an effort of the understanding to believe that they indeed form a part of the earth.

From this point we descended to Neuchâtel, which is situated in a narrow plain, between the mountains and its immense lake, and presents no additional aspect of peculiar interest.

We remained the following day at this town, occupied in a consideration of the step it would now be advisable for us to take. The money we had brought with us from Paris was nearly exhausted, but we obtained about £38 in silver upon discount from one of the bankers of the city, and with this we resolved to journey towards the Lake of Uri, and seek in that romantic and interesting country some cottage where we might dwell in peace and solitude. Such were our dreams, which we should probably have realised had it not been for the deficiency of that indispensable article money, which obliged us to return to England.

A Swiss, whom S. met at the post-office, kindly interested himself in our affairs, and assisted us to hire a *voiture* to convey us to Lucerne, the principal town of the Lake of that name, which is connected with the Lake of Uri. The journey to this place occupied rather more than two days. The country was flat and dull, and excepting that we now and then caught a glimpse of the divine Alps, there was nothing in it to interest us. Lucerne promised better things, and as soon as we arrived, (August 23rd,) we hired a boat, with which we proposed to coast the lake until we should meet with some suitable habitation, or perhaps even going to Altorf, cross Mont St. Gothard, and seek in the warm climate of the country to the south of the Alps an air more salubrious, and a temperature better fitted for the precarious state of S.' health than the bleak region to the north. The Lake of Lucerne is encompassed on all sides by high mountains that rise abruptly from the water; sometimes their bare fronts descend perpendicularly and cast a black shade upon the waves; sometimes they are covered with thick wood, whose dark foliage is interspersed by the brown bare crags on which the trees have taken root. In every part where a glade shows itself in the forest it appears cultivated, and cottages peep from among the woods. The most luxuriant islands, rocky and covered with moss and bending trees, are sprinkled over the lake. Most of these are decorated by the figure of a saint in wretched waxwork.

The direction of this lake extends first from east to west, then turning a right angle, it lies from north to south; this latter part is distinguished in name from the other, and is called the Lake of Uri. The former part is also nearly divided midway, where the jutting land almost meets, and its craggy sides cast a deep shadow on the little strait through which you pass. The summits of several of the mountains that inclose the lake to the south are covered by eternal glaciers.

Brunnen is situated on the northern side of the angle which the lake makes, forming the extremity of the Lake of Lucerne. Here we rested for the night, and dismissed our boatmen. Nothing could be more magnificent than the view from this spot. The high mountains encompassed us, darkening the waters; at a distance on the shores of Uri we could perceive the Chapel of Tell, and this was the village where he matured the conspiracy which was to overthrow the tyrant of his country; and indeed this lovely lake, these sublime mountains and wild forests, seemed a fit cradle for a mind aspiring to high adventure and heroic deeds. Yet we saw no glimpse of his spirit in his present countrymen. The Swiss appeared to us then, and experience has confirmed our opinion, a people slow of comprehension and of action; but habit has made them unfit for slavery, and they would, I have little doubt, make a brave defence against any invader of their freedom.

Such were our reflections, and we remained until late in the evening on the shores of the lake, conversing, enjoying the rising breeze, and contemplating with feelings of exquisite delight the divine objects that surrounded us.

The following day was spent in a consideration of our circumstances, and in contemplation of the scene around us. A furious *vent d'Italie*, (south wind,) tore up the lake, making immense waves, and carrying the water in a whirlwind high in the air, when it fell like heavy rain into the lake. The waves broke with a tremendous noise on the rocky shores. This conflict continued during the whole day, but it became calmer towards the evening. S. and I walked on the banks, and sitting on a rude pier, S. read aloud the account of the Siege of Jerusalem from Tacitus.

In the meantime we endeavoured to find an habitation, but could only procure two unfurnished rooms in an ugly big house, called the Château. These we hired at a guinea a month, had beds moved into them, and the next day took possession. But it was a wretched place, with no comfort or convenience. It was with difficulty that we could get any food prepared: as it was cold and rainy, we ordered a fire: they lighted an immense stove which occupied a corner of the room; it was long before it heated, and when hot, the warmth was so unwholesome that we were obliged to throw open our windows to prevent a kind of suffocation; added to this, there was but one person in Brunnen who could speak French, a barbarous kind of German being the language of this part of Switzerland. It was with difficulty, therefore, that we could get our most ordinary wants supplied.

These immediate inconveniences led us to a more serious consideration of our situation. The £28 which we possessed was all the money that we could count upon with any certainty, until the following December. S.' presence in London was absolutely necessary for the procuring any further supply. What were we to do? We should soon be reduced to absolute want. Thus after balancing the various topics that offered themselves for discussion, we resolved to return to England.

Having formed this resolution, we had not a moment for delay: our little store was sensibly decreasing, and £28 could hardly appear sufficient for so long a journey. It had cost us £60 to cross France from Paris to Neuchâtel; but we now resolved on a more economical mode of travelling. Water-conveyances are always the cheapest, and fortunately we were so situated, that by taking advantage of the rivers of the Reuss and Rhine we could reach England without travelling a league on land. This was our plan; we should travel eight hundred miles; and was this possible for so small a sum? But there was no other alternative, and indeed S. only knew how very little we had to depend upon.

We departed the next morning for the Town of Lucerne. It rained violently during the first part of our voyage, but towards its conclusion the sky became clear, and the sunbeams dried and cheered us. We saw again, and for the last time, the rocky shores of this beautiful lake, its verdant isles, and snow-capt mountains.

We landed at Lucerne, and remained in that town the following night, and the next morning, (August

27th,) departed in the *diligence-par-eau* for Loffenburg, a town on the Rhine, where the falls of that river prevented the same vessel from proceeding any farther. Our companions in this voyage were of the meanest class, smoked prodigiously, and were exceedingly disgusting. After having landed for refreshment in the middle of the day, we found, on our return to the boat, that our former seats were occupied; we took others, when the original possessors angrily, and almost with violence, insisted upon our leaving them. Their brutal rudeness to us, who did not understand their language, provoked S. to knock one of the foremost down: he did not return the blow, but continued his vociferations until the boatmen interfered, and provided us with other seats.

The Reuss is exceedingly rapid, and we descended several falls, one of more than eight feet. There is something very delicious in the sensation when at one moment you are at the top of a fall of water, and before the second has expired you are at the bottom, still rushing on with the impulse which the descent has given. The waters of the Rhone are blue, those of the Reuss are of a deep green. I should think that there must be something in the beds of these rivers, and that the accidents of the banks and sky cannot alone cause this difference.

Sleeping at Dettingen, we arrived the next morning at Loffenburg, where we engaged a small canoe to convey us to Mumph. I give these boats this Indian appellation, as they were of the rudest construction—long, narrow, and flat-bottomed: they consisted merely of straight pieces of deal board, unpainted, and nailed together with so little care that the water constantly poured in at the crevices, and the boat perpetually required emptying. The river was rapid, and sped swiftly, breaking as it passed on innumerable rocks just covered by the water; it was a sight of some dread to see our frail boat winding among the eddies of the rocks which it was death to touch, and when the slightest inclination on one side would instantly have overset it.

We could not procure a boat at Mumph, and we thought ourselves lucky in meeting with a return cabriolet to Rheinfelden. But our good fortune was of short duration; about a league from Mumph the cabriolet broke down, and we were obliged to proceed on foot. Fortunately we were overtaken by some Swiss soldiers, who were discharged and returning home, who carried our box for us as far as Rheinfelden, when we were directed to proceed a league farther to a village where boats were commonly hired. Here, although not without some difficulty, we procured a boat for Basle, and proceeded down a swift river, while evening came on, and the air was bleak and comfortless. Our voyage was, however, short, and we arrived at the place of our destination by six in the evening.

V. GERMANY

BEFORE we slept, S. had made a bargain for a boat to carry us to Mayence, and the next morning, bidding adieu to Switzerland, we embarked in a boat laden with merchandise, but where we had no fellow-passengers to disturb our tranquillity by their vulgarity and rudeness. The wind was violently against us, but the stream, aided by a slight exertion from the rowers, carried us on; the sun shone pleasantly, S. read aloud to us "Mary Wollstonecraft's Letters from Norway," and we passed our time delightfully.

The evening was such as to find few parallels in beauty; as it approached, the banks, which had hitherto been flat and uninteresting, became exceedingly beautiful. Suddenly the river grew narrow, and the boat dashed with inconceivable rapidity round the base of a rocky hill covered with pines; a ruined tower, with its desolated windows, stood on the summit of another hill that jutted into the river; beyond, the sunset was illuminating the distant mountains and clouds, casting the reflection of its rich and purple hues on the agitated river. The brilliance and contrasts of the colours on the circling whirlpools of the stream was an appearance entirely new and most beautiful; the shades grew darker as the sun descended below the horizon, and after we had landed, as we walked to our inn round a beautiful bay, the full moon arose with divine splendour, casting its silver light on the before-purpled waves.

The following morning we pursued our journey in a slight canoe, in which every motion was accompanied with danger; but the stream had lost much of its rapidity, and was no longer impeded by rocks, the banks were low and covered with willows. We passed Strasburg, and the next morning it was proposed to us that we should proceed in the *diligence-par-eau*, as the navigation would become dangerous for our small boat.

There were only four passengers besides ourselves. Three of these were students of the Strasburg University: Schwitz, a rather handsome, good-tempered young man; Hoff, a kind of shapeless animal, with a heavy ugly German face; and Schneider, who was nearly an idiot, and on whom his companions were always playing a thousand tricks. The remaining passengers were a woman and an infant.

The country was uninteresting, but we enjoyed

CASTLE OF RHEINSTEIN

fine weather, and slept in the boat in the open air without any inconvenience. We saw on the shores few objects that called forth our attention, if I except the town of Mannheim, which was strikingly neat and clean. It was situated at about a mile from the river, and the road to it was planted on each side with beautiful acacias. The last part of this voyage was performed close under land, as the wind was so violently against us that, even with all the force of a rapid current in our favour, we were hardly permitted to proceed. We were told, (and not without reason,) that we ought to congratulate ourselves on having exchanged our canoe for this boat, as the river was now of considerable width, and tossed by the wind into large waves. The same morning a boat, containing fifteen persons, in attempting to cross the water, had upset in the middle of the river, and every one in it perished. We saw the boat, turned over, floating down the stream. This was a melancholy sight, yet ludicrously commented on by the *Batelier;* almost the whole stock of whose French consisted in the word "*seulement.*" When we asked him what had happened, he answered, laying particular emphasis on this favourite dissyllable, "*C'est seulement un bateau, qui était seulement renversé, et tous les peuples sont seulement noyés.*"

Mayence is one of the best fortified towns in

Germany. The river, which is broad and rapid, guards it to the east, and the hills for three leagues around exhibit signs of fortifications. The town itself is old, the streets narrow, and the houses high: the cathedral and towers of the town still bear marks of the bombardment which took place in the Revolutionary War.

We took our places in the *diligence-par-eau* for Cologne, and the next morning (September 4th) departed. This conveyance appeared much more like a mercantile English affair than any we had before seen; it was shaped like a steamboat, with a cabin and a high deck. Most of our companions chose to remain in the cabin; this was fortunate for us, since nothing could be more horribly disgusting than the lower order of smoking drinking Germans who travelled with us; they swaggered and talked, and what was hideous to English eyes, kissed one another: there were, however, two or three merchants of a better class, who appeared well-informed and polite.

The part of the Rhine down which we now glided is that so beautifully described by Lord Byron in his Third Canto of "Childe Harold." We read these verses with delight, as they conjured before us these lovely scenes with the truth and vividness of painting, and with the exquisite addition of glowing language and a warm imagination. We were carried down by a dangerously rapid current, and saw on either side of us hills covered with vines and trees, craggy cliffs crowned by desolate towers, and wooded islands where picturesque ruins peeped from behind the foliage, and cast the shadows of their forms on the troubled waters which distorted without deforming them. We heard the songs of the vintagers, and if the sight was not so replete with enjoyment as I now fancy it to have been; yet memory, taking all the dark shades from the picture, presents this part of the Rhine to my remembrance as the loveliest paradise on earth.

We had sufficient leisure for the enjoyment of these scenes, for the boatmen, neither rowing nor steering, suffered us to be carried down by the stream, and the boat turned round and round as it descended.

While I speak with disgust of the Germans who travelled with us, I should in justice to these Borderers record, that at one of the inns here we saw the only pretty woman we met with in the course of our travels. She is what I should conceive to be a truly German beauty; grey eyes, slightly tinged with brown, and expressive of uncommon sweetness and frankness. She had lately recovered from a fever, and this added to the interest of her countenance by adorning it with an appearance of extreme delicacy.

On the following day we left the hills of the Rhine, and found that for the remainder of our journey we should move sluggishly through the flats of Holland: the river also winds extremely, so that after calculating our resources we resolved to finish our journey in a land-diligence. Our water-conveyance remained that night at Bonn, and that we might lose no time, we proceeded post the same night to Cologne, where we arrived late; for the rate of travelling in Germany seldom exceeds a mile and a half an hour.

Cologne appeared an immense town as we drove through street after street to arrive at our inn. Before we slept we secured places in the diligence, which was to depart next morning for Cleves.

Nothing in the world can be more wretched than travelling in this German diligence: the coach is clumsy and comfortless, and we proceeded so slowly, stopping so often, that it appeared as if we should never arrive at our journey's end. We were allowed two hours for dinner, and two more were wasted in the evening while the coach was being changed. We were then requested, as the diligence had a greater demand for places than it could supply, to proceed in a cabriole, which was provided for us. We readily consented, as we hoped to travel faster than in the heavy diligence; but this was not permitted, and we jogged on all night behind this cumbrous machine.

In the morning we stopped, and for a moment indulged a hope that we had arrived at Cleves, which was at the distance of five leagues from our last night's stage; but we had only advanced three leagues in seven or eight hours, and had yet eight miles to perform. However, we first rested about three hours at this stage, where we could not obtain breakfast or any convenience, and at about eight o'clock we again departed, and with slow although far from easy travelling, faint with hunger and fatigue, we arrived by noon at Cleves.

VI. HOLLAND

Tired by the slow pace of the diligence, we resolved to post the remainder of the way. We had now, however, left Germany, and travelled at about the same rate as an English post-chaise. The country was entirely flat, and the roads so sandy, that the horses proceeded with difficulty. The only ornaments of this country are the turf fortifications that surround the towns. At Nimeguen we passed the flying bridge, mentioned in the letters of Lady Mary Montague. We had intended to travel all night, but at Tiel, where we arrived at about ten o'clock, we were assured that no post-boy was to be found who would proceed at so late an hour, on account of the robbers who infested the roads. This was an obvious imposition; but as we could procure neither horses nor driver, we were obliged to sleep here.

During the whole of the following day the road lay between canals, which intersect this country in every direction. The roads were excellent, but the Dutch have contrived as many inconveniences as possible. In our journey of the day before, we had passed by a windmill, which was so situated with regard to the road, that it was only by keeping close to the opposite side and passing quickly that we could avoid the sweep of its sails.

The roads between the canals were only wide enough to admit of one carriage, so that when we encountered another we were obliged sometimes to back for half a mile, until we should come to one of the drawbridges which led to the fields, on which one of the cabriolets was rolled, while the other passed. But they have another practice which is still more annoying: the flax when cut is put to soak under the mud of the canals, and then placed to dry against the trees which are planted on either side of the road; the stench that it exhales, when the beams of the sun draw out the moisture, is scarcely endurable. We saw many enormous frogs and toads in the canals; and the only sight which refreshed the eye by its beauty was the delicious verdure of the fields, where the grass was as rich and green as that of England, an appearance not common on the Continent.

Rotterdam is remarkably clean: the Dutch even wash the outside brickwork of their houses. We remained here one day, and met with a man in a very unfortunate condition: he had been born in Holland, and had spent so much of his life between England, France, and Germany, that he had acquired a slight knowledge of the language of each country, and spoke all very imperfectly. He said that he understood English best, but he was nearly unable to express himself in that.

On the evening of the 8th of August [September] we sailed from Rotterdam, but contrary winds obliged us to remain nearly two days at Maasluys, a town about two leagues from Rotterdam. Here our last guinea was expended, and we reflected with wonder that we had travelled eight hundred miles for less than thirty pounds, passing through lovely scenes, and enjoying the beauteous Rhine and all the brilliant shows of earth and sky, perhaps more, travelling as we did in an open boat, than if we had been shut up in a carriage and passed on the road under the hills.

The Captain of our vessel was an Englishman, and had been a King's Pilot. The bar of the Rhine [Maas] a little below Maasluys is so dangerous that without a very favourable **breeze** none of the Dutch vessels **dare** attempt its **passage**; but although the wind was **a very few** points in our favour, our Captain resolved **to sail, and** although half repentant before he had accomplished his undertaking, he was glad and proud when, triumphing over the timorous Dutchmen, the bar was crossed, and the vessel safe in the open sea. It was in truth an enterprise of some peril; a heavy **gale** had prevailed during the night, and although it had abated since the morning, the breakers at the **bar were** still exceedingly high. Through some **delay, which had arisen** from the ship having got aground in the harbour, we arrived half an hour after the appointed time. The breakers were tremendous, and we were informed **that** there was the space **of** only two feet between the bottom of the vessel and the sands. The waves, which broke against the **sides of** the ship with a terrible shock, were quite perpendicular, and even sometimes overhanging in the abrupt smoothness of their sides. Shoals of enormous porpoises were sporting with the utmost composure amidst the troubled waters.

We safely passed this danger, and after a navigation unexpectedly **short, arrived at Gravesend on** the morning of the 13th of September, **the** third day after **our departure** from Maasluys. M.

LETTERS WRITTEN DURING A RESIDENCE OF THREE MONTHS IN THE ENVIRONS OF GENEVA, IN THE SUMMER OF THE YEAR 1816.

LETTER I

Hôtel de Sècheron, Geneva,
May 17, 1816.

WE arrived at Paris on the 8th of this month, and were detained two days for the purpose of obtaining the various signatures necessary to our passports, the French Government having become much more circumspect since the escape of Lavalette. We had no letters of introduction or any friend in that city, and were therefore confined to our hotel, where we were obliged to hire apartments for the week, although when we first arrived we expected to be detained one night only; for in Paris there are no houses where you can be accommodated with apartments by the day.

The manners of the French are interesting,

although less attractive, at least to Englishmen, than before the last invasion of the Allies: the discontent and sullenness of their minds perpetually betrays itself. Nor is it wonderful that they should regard the subjects of a government which fills their country with hostile garrisons, and sustains a detested dynasty on the throne, with an acrimony and indignation of which that government alone is the proper object. This feeling is honourable to the French, and encouraging to all those of every nation in Europe who have a fellow-feeling with the oppressed, and who cherish an unconquerable hope that the cause of liberty must at length prevail.

Our route after Paris, as far as Troyes, lay through the same uninteresting tract of country which we had traversed on foot nearly two years before, but on quitting Troyes we left the road leading to Neuchâtel, to follow that which was to conduct us to Geneva. We entered Dijon on the third evening after our departure from Paris, and passing through Dôle, arrived at Poligny. This town is built at the foot of Jura, which rises abruptly from a plain of vast extent. The rocks of the mountain overhang the houses. Some difficulty in procuring horses detained us here until the evening closed in, when we proceeded by the light of a stormy moon to Champagnolles, a little village situated in the depths of the mountains. The road was serpentine and exceedingly steep, and was overhung on one side by half-distinguished precipices, whilst the other was a gulf filled by the darkness of the driving clouds. The dashing of the invisible mountain streams announced to us that we had quitted the plains of France, as we slowly ascended, amidst a violent storm of wind and rain, to Champagnolles, where we arrived at twelve o'clock, the fourth night after our departure from Paris.

The next morning we proceeded, still ascending among the ravines and valleys of the mountain. The scenery perpetually grows more wonderful and sublime: pine forests, of impenetrable thickness and untrodden, nay inaccessible expanse, spread on every side. Sometimes the dark woods descending follow the route into the valleys, the distorted trees struggling with knotted roots between the most barren clefts; sometimes the road winds high into the regions of frost, and then the forests become scattered, and the branches of the trees are loaded with snow, and half of the enormous pines themselves buried in the wavy drifts. The Spring, as the inhabitants informed us, was unusually late, and indeed the cold was excessive; as we ascended the mountains, the same clouds which rained on us in the valleys poured forth large flakes of snow thick and fast. The sun occasionally shone through these showers, and illuminated the magnificent ravines of the mountains, whose gigantic pines were some laden with snow, some wreathed round by the lines of scattered and lingering vapour, others darting their dark spires into the sunny sky, brilliantly clear and azure.

As the evening advanced, and we ascended higher, the snow, which we had beheld whitening the overhanging rocks, now encroached upon our road, and it snowed fast as we entered the village of Les Rousses, where we were threatened by the apparent necessity of passing the night in a bad inn and dirty beds. For from that place there are two roads to Geneva; one by Nion, in the Swiss territory, where the mountain route is shorter, and comparatively easy at that time of the year, when the road is for several leagues covered with snow of an enormous depth; the other road lay through Gex, and was too circuitous and dangerous to be attempted at so late an hour in the day. Our passport, however, was for Gex, and we were told that we could not change its destination; but all these police laws, so severe in themselves, are to be softened by bribery, and this difficulty was at length overcome. We hired four horses, and ten men to support the carriage, and departed from Les Rousses at six in the evening, when the sun had already far descended, and the snow pelting against the windows of our carriage, assisted the coming darkness to deprive us of the view of the Lake of Geneva and the far-distant Alps.

The prospect around, however, was sufficiently sublime to command our attention: never was scene more awfully desolate. The trees in these regions are incredibly large, and stand in scattered clumps over the white wilderness; the vast expanse of snow was chequered only by these gigantic pines and the poles that marked our road: no river or rock-encircled lawn relieved the eye, by adding the picturesque to the sublime. The natural silence of that uninhabited desert contrasted strangely with the voices of the men who conducted us, who with animated tones and gestures called to one another in a *patois* composed of French and Italian, creating disturbance where but for them there was none.

To what a different scene are we now arrived! To the warm sunshine and to the humming of sun-loving insects. From the windows of our hotel we see the lovely lake, blue as the heavens which it reflects, and sparkling with golden beams. The opposite shore is sloping, and covered with vines, which however do not so early in the season add to the beauty of the prospect. Gentlemen's seats are scattered over these banks, behind which rise the various ridges of black mountains, and towering far above, in the midst of its snowy Alps, the majestic Mont Blanc, highest and queen of all. Such is the view reflected by the lake; it is a bright summer scene without any of that sacred solitude and deep seclusion that delighted us at Lucerne.

We have not yet found out any very agreeable walks, but you know our attachment to water excursions. We have hired a boat, and every evening at about six o'clock we sail on the lake, which is delightful, whether we glide over a glassy surface or are speeded along by a strong wind. The waves of this lake never afflict me with that sickness that deprives me of all enjoyment in a sea voyage; on the contrary, the tossing of our boat raises my spirits and inspires me with unusual hilarity. Twilight here is of short duration, but we at present enjoy the benefit of an increasing moon, and seldom return until ten o'clock, when, as we approach the shore, we are saluted by the delightful scent of flowers and new-mown grass, and the chirp of the grasshoppers, and the song of the evening birds.

We do not enter into society here, yet our time passes swiftly and delightfully. We read Latin and Italian during the heats of noon, and when the sun declines we walk in the garden of the hotel, looking at the rabbits, relieving fallen cockchafers, and watching the motions of a myriad of lizards, who inhabit a southern wall of the garden. You know that we have just escaped from the gloom of winter and of London; and coming to this delightful spot during this divine weather, I feel as happy as a new-fledged bird, and hardly care what twig I fly to, so that I may try my new-found wings. A more experienced bird may be more difficult in its choice of a bower; but in my present temper of mind, the budding flowers, the fresh grass of spring, and the happy creatures about me that live and enjoy these pleasures, are quite enough to afford me exquisite delight, even though clouds should shut out Mont Blanc from my sight. Adieu! M.

LETTER II

Campagne C. (Chapuis), near Coligny,
June 1.

You will perceive from my date that we have changed our residence since my last. We now inhabit a little cottage on the opposite shore of the lake, and have exchanged the view of Mont Blanc and her snowy Aiguilles for the dark frowning Jura, behind whose range we every evening see the sun sink, and darkness approaches our valley from behind the Alps, which are then tinged by the glowing rose-like hue which is observed in England to attend on the clouds of an autumnal sky when daylight is almost gone. The lake is at our feet, and a little harbour contains our boat, in which we still enjoy our evening excursions on the water. Unfortunately we do not now enjoy those brilliant skies that hailed us on our first arrival to this country. An almost perpetual rain confines us principally to the house; but when the sun bursts forth it is with a splendour and heat unknown in England. The thunder-storms that visit us are grander and more terrific than I have ever seen before. We watch them as they approach from the opposite side of the lake, observing the lightning play among the clouds in various parts of the heavens and dart in jagged figures upon the piny heights of Jura, dark with the shadow of the overhanging cloud, while perhaps the sun is shining cheerily upon us. One night we enjoyed a finer storm than I had ever before beheld. The lake was lit up, the pines on Jura made visible, and all the scene illuminated for an instant, when a pitchy blackness succeeded, and the thunder came in frightful bursts over our heads amid the darkness.

But while I still dwell on the country around Geneva, you will expect me to say something of the town itself: there is nothing, however, in it that can repay you for the trouble of walking over its rough stones. The houses are high, the streets narrow, many of them on the ascent, and no public building of any beauty to attract your eye, or any architecture to gratify your taste. The town is surrounded by a wall, the three gates of which are shut exactly at ten o'clock, when no bribery (as in France) can open them. To the south of the town is the promenade of the Genevese, a grassy plain planted with a few trees and called Plainpalais. . . . Another Sunday recreation for the citizens is an excursion to the top of Mont Salève. This hill is within a league of the town, and rises perpendicularly from the cultivated plain. It is ascended on the other side, and I should judge from its situation that your toil is rewarded by a delightful view of the course of the Rhone and Arve and of the shores of the lake. We have not yet visited it.

There is more equality of classes here than in England. This occasions a greater freedom and refinement of manners among the lower orders than we meet with in our own country. The peasants of Switzerland may not, however, emulate the vivacity and grace of the French. They are more cleanly, but they are slow and inapt. I know a girl of twenty, who although she had lived all her life among vineyards, could not inform me during what month the vintage took place, and I discovered she was utterly ignorant of the order in which the months succeed to one another. She would not have been surprised if I had talked of the burning sun and delicious fruits of December, or of the frosts of July. Yet she is by no means deficient in understanding.

The Genevese are also much inclined to Puritanism. It is true that from habit they dance on a Sunday, but as soon as the French Government was abolished in the town, the Magistrates ordered the theatre to be closed, and measures were taken to pull down the building.

We have latterly enjoyed fine weather, and nothing is more pleasant than to listen to the evening song of the vine-dressers. They are all women, and most of them have harmonious although masculine voices. The theme of their ballads consists of shepherds, love, flocks, and the sons of kings who fall in love with beautiful shepherdesses. Their tunes are monotonous, but it is sweet to hear them in the stillness of the evening, while we are enjoying the sight of the setting sun, either from the hill behind our house or from the lake.

Such are our pleasures here, which would be greatly increased if the season had been more favourable, for they chiefly consist in such enjoyments as sunshine and gentle breezes bestow. We have

not yet made any excursion in the environs of the town, but we have planned several, when you shall again hear of us: and we will endeavour, by the magic of words, to transport the ethereal part of you to the neighbourhood of the Alps and mountain-streams, and forests, which while they clothe the former darken the latter with their vast shadows. Adieu!
                                          M.

LETTER III

To T. P., Esq.

Montalègre, near Coligny, Geneva.
July 12.

IT is nearly a fortnight since I have returned from Vevey. . . . But I will give you an abstract of our voyage, which lasted eight days, and if you have a map of Switzerland, you can follow me.

We left Montalègre at half-past two on the 23rd of June. The lake was calm, and after three hours of rowing we arrived at Hermance, a beautiful little village containing a ruined tower, built, the villagers say, by Julius Cæsar. There were three other towers similar to it, which the Genevese destroyed for their own fortifications in 1560. We got into the tower by a kind of window. The walls are immensely solid, and the stone of which it is built so hard that it yet retained the mark of chisels. The boatmen said that this tower was once three times higher than it is now. There are two staircases in the thickness of the walls, one of which is entirely demolished, and the other half-ruined and only accessible by a ladder. The town itself, now an inconsiderable village inhabited by a few fishermen, was built by a Queen of Burgundy, and reduced to its present state by the inhabitants of Berne, who burnt and ravaged everything they could find.

Leaving Hermance, we arrived at sunset at the village of Nerni. After looking at our lodgings, which were gloomy and dirty, we walked out by the side of the lake. It was beautiful to see the vast expanse of these purple and misty waters broken by the craggy islets near to its slant and " beachèd margin." There were many fish sporting in the lake, and multitudes were collected close to the rocks to catch the flies which inhabited them.

On returning to the village, we sat on a wall beside the lake, looking at some children who were playing at a game like ninepins. The children here appeared in an extraordinary way deformed and diseased. Most of them were crooked, and with enlarged throats; but one little boy had such exquisite grace in his mien and motions as I never before saw equalled in a child. His countenance was beautiful for the expression with which it overflowed. There was a mixture of pride and gentleness in his eyes and lips, the indications of sensibility, which his education will probably pervert to misery or seduce to crime; but there was more of gentleness than of pride, and it seemed that the pride was tamed from its original wildness by the habitual exercise of milder feelings. My companion gave him a piece of money, which he took without speaking, with a sweet smile of easy thankfulness, and then with an unembarrassed air turned to his play. All this might scarcely be; but the imagination surely could not forbear to breathe into the most inanimate forms some likeness of its own visions, on such a serene and glowing evening, in this remote and romantic village, beside the calm lake that bore us hither.

On returning to our inn, we found that the servant had arranged our rooms, and deprived them of the greater portion of their former disconsolate appearance. They reminded my companion of Greece: it was five years, he said, since he had slept in such beds. The influence of the recollections excited by this circumstance on our conversation gradually faded, and I retired to rest with no unpleasant sensations, thinking of our journey to-morrow, and of the pleasure of recounting the little adventures of it when we return.

The next morning we passed Yvoire, a scattered village with an ancient castle, whose houses are interspersed with trees, and which stands at a little distance from Nerni, on the promontory which bounds a deep bay some miles in extent. So soon as we arrived at this promontory, the lake began to assume an aspect of wilder magnificence. The Mountains of Savoy, whose summits were bright with snow, descended in broken slopes to the lake: on high, the rocks were dark with pine-forests, which become deeper and more immense, until the ice and snow mingle with the points of naked rock that pierce the blue air; but below, groves of walnut, chestnut, and oak, with openings of lawny fields, attested the milder climate.

As soon as we had passed the opposite promontory, we saw the River Drance, which descends from between a chasm in the mountains, and makes a plain near the lake, intersected by its divided streams. Thousands of *Besolets*, beautiful waterbirds, like sea-gulls, but smaller, with purple on their backs, take their station on the shallows, where its waters mingle with the lake. As we approached Evian, the mountains descended more precipitously to the lake, and masses of intermingled wood and rock overhung its shining spire.

We arrived at this town about seven o'clock, after

a day which involved more rapid changes of atmosphere than I ever recollect to have observed before. The morning was cold and wet; then an easterly wind, and the clouds hard and high; then thunder showers, and wind shifting to every quarter; then a warm blast from the south, and summer clouds hanging over the peaks, with bright blue sky between. About half an hour after we had arrived at Evian, a few flashes of lightning came fron a dark cloud directly overhead, and continued after the cloud had dispersed.

The appearance of the inhabitants of Evian is more wretched, diseased, and poor, than I ever recollect to have seen. The contrast indeed between the subjects of the King of Sardinia and the citizens of the independent republics of Switzerland, affords a powerful illustration of the blighting mischiefs of despotism, within the space of a few miles. They have mineral waters here: "*Eaux savonneuses*," they call them. In the evening we had some difficulty about our passports, but so soon as the Syndic heard my companion's rank and name, he apologised for the circumstance. The inn was good. During our voyage, on the distant height of a hill covered with pine-forests, we saw a ruined castle which reminded me of those on the Rhine.

We left Evian on the following morning, with a

wind of such violence as to permit but one sail to be carried. The waves also were exceedingly high, and our boat so heavily laden, that there appeared to be some danger. We arrived however safe at Meillerie, after passing with great speed mighty forests which overhung the lake, and lawns of exquisite verdure, and mountains with bare and icy points, which rose immediately from the summit of the rocks, whose bases were echoing to the waves. . . .

We dined there, and had some honey, the best I have ever tasted, the very essence of the mountain-flowers, and as fragrant. Probably the village derives its name from this production. . . . Groves of pine, chestnut, and walnut overshadow it; magnificent and unbounded forests to which England affords no parallel. In the midst of these woods are dells of lawny expanse, inconceivably verdant, adorned with a thousand of the rarest flowers and odorous with thyme.

The lake appeared somewhat calmer as we left Meillerie, sailing close to the banks, whose magnificence augmented with the turn of every promontory. But we congratulated ourselves too soon: the wind gradually increased in violence, until it blew tremendously; and as it came from the remotest extremity of the lake, produced waves of a frightful height, and covered the whole surface with a chaos of foam. One of our boatmen, who was a dreadfully stupid fellow, persisted in holding the sail at a time when the boat was on the point of being driven under water by the hurricane. On discovering his error, he let it entirely go, and the boat for a moment refused to obey the helm; in addition, the rudder was so broken as to render the management of it very difficult; one wave fell in, and then another. My companion, an excellent swimmer, took off his coat, I did the same, and we sat with our arms crossed, every instant expecting to be swamped. The sail was however again held, the boat obeyed the helm, and still in imminent peril from the immensity of the waves, we arrived in a few minutes at a sheltered port, in the village of St. Gingoux.

I felt in this near prospect of death a mixture of sensations, among which terror entered, though but subordinately. My feelings would have been less painful had I been alone; but I know that my companion would have attempted to save me, and I was overcome with humiliation, when I thought that his life might have been risked to preserve mine. When we arrived at St. Gingoux, the inhabitants, who stood on the shore, unaccustomed to see a vessel as frail as ours, and fearing to venture at all on such a sea, exchanged looks of wonder and congratulation with our boatmen, who as well as ourselves were well pleased to set foot on shore.

St. Gingoux is even more beautiful than Meillerie; the mountains are higher, and their loftiest points of elevation descend more abruptly to the lake. On high, the aërial summits still cherish great depths of snow in their ravines, and in the paths of their unseen torrents. One of the highest of these is called Roche de St. Julien, beneath whose pinnacles the forests become deeper and more extensive; the chestnut gives a peculiarity to the scene, which is most beautiful, and will make a picture in my memory, distinct from all other mountain scenes which I have ever before visited.

As we arrived here early, we took a *voiture* to visit the mouth of the Rhone. We went between the mountains and the lake, under groves of mighty chestnut-trees, beside perpetual streams, which are nourished by the snows above and form stalactites on the rocks over which they fall. We saw an immense chestnut-tree which had been overthrown by the hurricane of the morning. The place where the Rhone joins the lake was marked by a line of tremendous breakers; the river is as rapid as when it leaves the lake, but is muddy and dark. We went about a league farther on the road to La Valais, and stopped at a castle called La Tour de Bouverie, which seems to be the frontier of Switzerland and Savoy, as we were asked for our passports, on the supposition of our proceeding to Italy.

On one side of the road was the immense Roche de St. Julien, which overhung it; through the gateway of the castle we saw the snowy mountains of La Valais, clothed in clouds, and on the other side was the willowy plain of the Rhone, in a character of striking contrast with the rest of the scene, bounded by the dark mountains that overhang Clarens, Vevey, and the lake that rolls between. In the midst of the plain rises a little isolated hill, on which the white spire of a church peeps from among the tufted chestnut woods.

As my companion rises late, I had time before breakfast, on the ensuing morning, to hunt the waterfalls of the river that fall into the lake at St. Gingoux. The stream is indeed, from the declivity over which it falls, only a succession of waterfalls, which roar over the rocks with a perpetual sound, and suspend their unceasing spray on the leaves and flowers that overhang and adorn its savage banks. The path that conducted along this river sometimes avoided the precipices of its shores, by leading through meadows; sometimes threaded the base of the perpendicular and caverned rocks. I gathered in these meadows a nosegay of such flowers as I never saw in England, and which I thought more beautiful for that rarity.

On my return, after breakfast, we sailed for Clarens, determining first to see the three mouths of the Rhone, and then the Castle of Chillon; the day was fine, and the water calm. We passed from the blue waters of the lake over the stream of the Rhone, which is rapid even at a great distance from its confluence with the lake; the turbid waters mixed with those of the lake, but mixed with them unwillingly. . . .

We passed on to the Castle of Chillon, and visited its dungeons and towers. These prisons are excavated below the lake; the principal dungeon is supported by seven columns, whose branching capitals support the roof. Close to the very walls, the lake is eight hundred feet deep; iron rings are fastened to these columns, and on them were engraven a multitude of names, partly those of visitors, and partly doubtless of the prisoners, of whom now no memory remains, and who thus beguiled a solitude which they have long ceased to feel. One date was as ancient as 1670.

Close to this long and lofty dungeon was a narrow cell, and beyond it one larger and far more lofty and dark, supported upon two unornamented arches.

Across one of these arches was a beam, now black and rotten, on which prisoners were hung in secret. I never saw a monument more terrible of that cold and inhuman tyranny, which it has been the delight of man to exercise over man. . . . The *Gendarme*, who conducted us over this castle, told us that there was an opening to the lake, by means of a secret spring, connected with which the whole dungeon might be filled with water before the prisoners could possibly escape.

We proceeded with a contrary wind to Clarens, against a heavy swell. I never felt more strongly than on landing at Clarens, that the spirit of old times had deserted its once cherished habitation. . . .

On the following day we went to see the Castle of Clarens, a square strong house, with very few windows, surrounded by a double terrace that overlooks the valley, or rather the plain of Clarens. The road which conducted to it wound up the steep ascent through woods of walnut and chestnut. . . .

We sailed from Clarens to Vevey. Vevey is a town more beautiful in its simplicity than any I have ever seen. Its market-place, a spacious square interspersed with trees, looks directly upon the mountains of Savoy and La Valais, the Lake and the Valley of the Rhone. . . . From Vevey we came to Ouchy, a village near Lausanne. The coasts of the

Pays de Vaud, though full of villages and vineyards, present an aspect of tranquillity and peculiar beauty which well compensates for the solitude which I am accustomed to admire. The hills are very high and rocky, crowned and interspersed with woods. Waterfalls echo from the cliffs, and shine afar. In one place we saw the traces of two rocks of immense size, which had fallen from the mountain behind. One of these lodged in a room where a young woman was sleeping, without injuring her. The vineyards were utterly destroyed in its path, and the earth torn up.

The rain detained us two days at Ouchy. We however visited Lausanne, and saw Gibbon's house. We were shown the decayed summer-house where he finished his History, and the old acacias on the terrace, from which he saw Mont Blanc, after having written the last sentence. There is something grand, and even touching, in the regret which he expresses at the completion of his task. It was conceived amid the ruins of the Capitol. The sudden departure of his cherished and accustomed toil must have left him, like the death of a dear friend, sad and solitary. . . . When we returned, in the only interval of sunshine during the day, I walked on the pier, which the lake was lashing with its waves. A rainbow spanned the lake, or rather rested one extremity of its arch upon the water and the other at the foot of the Mountains of Savoy. Some white houses, I know not if they were those of Meillerie, shone through the yellow fire.

On Saturday the 30th of June we quitted Ouchy, and after two days of pleasant sailing arrived on Sunday evening at Montalègre.

S.

LETTER IV

To T. P., Esq.

Hôtel de Londres, Chamouni,
July 22, 1816.

WHILST you, my friend, are engaged in securing a home for us, we are wandering in search of recollections to embellish it. I do not err in conceiving that you are interested in details of all that is majestic or beautiful in nature; but how shall I describe to you the scenes by which I am now surrounded? To exhaust the epithets which express the astonishment and the admiration, the very excess of satisfied astonishment where expectation scarcely acknowledged any boundary, is this to impress upon your mind the images which fill mine now even till it overflow? I too have read the raptures of travellers; I will be warned by their example; I will simply detail to you all that I can relate, or all that, if related, would enable you to conceive of what we have done or seen since the morning of the 20th, when we left Geneva.

We commenced our intended journey to Chamouni at half-past eight in the morning. We passed through the champaign country, which extends from Mont Salève to the base of the higher Alps. The country is sufficiently fertile, covered with corn-fields and orchards, and intersected by sudden acclivities with flat summits. The day was cloudless and excessively hot, the Alps were perpetually in sight, and as we advanced, the mountains which form their outskirts closed in around us. We passed a bridge over a stream which discharges itself into the Arve. The Arve itself, much swollen by the rains, flows constantly to the right of the road.

As we approached Bonneville through an avenue composed of a beautiful species of drooping poplar, we observed that the corn-fields on each side were covered with inundation. Bonneville is a neat little town, with no conspicuous peculiarity, except the white towers of the prison, an extensive building overlooking the town. At Bonneville the Alps commence, one of which, clothed by forests, rises almost immediately from the opposite bank of the Arve.

From Bonneville to Cluses the road conducts through a spacious and fertile plain, surrounded on all sides by mountains, covered like those of Meillerie with forests of intermingled pine and chestnut. At Cluses the road turns suddenly to the right, following the Arve along the chasm which it seems to have hollowed for itself among the perpendicular mountains. The scene assumes here a more savage and colossal character: the valley becomes narrow, affording no more space than is sufficient for the river and the road. The pines descend to the banks, imitating with their irregular spires the pyramidal crags which lift themselves far above the regions of forest into the deep azure of the sky and among the white dazzling clouds. The scene, at the distance of half a mile from Cluses, differs from that of Matlock in little else than in the immensity of its proportions, and in its untameable inaccessible solitude, inhabited only by the goats which we saw browsing on the rocks.

Near Magland, within a league of each other, we saw two waterfalls. They were no more than mountain rivulets, but the height from which they fell, at least of twelve hundred feet, made them assume a character inconsistent with the smallness of their stream. The first fell from the overhanging brow of a black precipice on an enormous rock, precisely resembling some colossal Egyptian statue of a female deity. It struck the head of the visionary image, and gracefully dividing there, fell from it in folds of foam more like to cloud than water, imitating a veil of the most exquisite woof. It then united, concealing the lower part of the statue, and hiding itself in a winding of its channel, burst into a deeper fall, and crossed our route in its path towards the Arve.

The other waterfall was more continuous and larger. The violence with which it fell made it look more like some shape which an exhalation had assumed, than like water, for it streamed beyond the mountain, which appeared dark behind it, as it might have appeared behind an evanescent cloud.

The character of the scenery continued the same until we arrived at St. Martin, (called in the maps Sallanches,) the mountains perpetually becoming more elevated, exhibiting at every turn of the road more craggy summits, loftier and wider extent of forests, darker and more deep recesses.

The following morning we proceeded from St. Martin on mules to Chamouni, accompanied by two guides. We proceeded, as we had done the preceding day, along the valley of the Arve, a valley surrounded on all sides by immense mountains, whose rugged precipices are intermixed on high with dazzling snow. Their bases were still covered with the eternal forests, which perpetually grew darker

CLUSE

and more profound as we approached the inner regions of the mountains.

On arriving at a small village, at the distance of a league from St. Martin, we dismounted from our mules, and were conducted by our guides to view a cascade. We beheld an immense body of water fall two hundred and fifty feet, dashing from rock to rock, and casting a spray which formed a mist around it, in the midst of which hung a multitude of sun-bows which faded or became unspeakably vivid as the inconstant sun shone through the clouds. When we approached near to it the rain of the spray reached us, and our clothes were wetted by the quick-falling but minute particles of water. The cataract fell from above into a deep craggy chasm at our feet, where changing its character to that of a mountain stream it pursued its course towards the Arve, roaring over the rocks that impeded its progress.

As we proceeded, our route still lay through the valley, or rather, as it had now become, the vast ravine which is at once the couch and the creation of the terrible Arve. We ascended, winding between mountains whose immensity staggers the imagination. We crossed the path of a torrent, which three days since had descended from the thawing snow and torn the road away.

We dined at Servoz, a little village where there are

lead and copper mines, and where we saw a cabinet of **natural curiosities,** like those of Keswick and Bethgelert. We saw in this cabinet some chamois' horns, and the horns of an exceedingly rare animal called the *bouquetin*, which inhabits the deserts of snow to the south of Mont Blanc: it is an animal of the stag kind; its horns weigh at least twenty-seven English pounds. It is inconceivable how so small an animal could support so inordinate a weight. The horns are of a very peculiar conformation, being broad, massy, and pointed at the ends, and surrounded with a number of rings which are supposed to afford an indication of its age: there were seventeen rings on the largest of these horns.

From Servoz three leagues remain to Chamouni. Mont Blanc **was** before us, the Alps with their innumerable glaciers on high all around closing in **the** complicated windings of the single vale: forests inexpressibly beautiful, but majestic in their beauty, intermingled beech and pine and oak, overshadowed our road or **receded**: whilst lawns, of such verdure as I have never seen before, occupied these openings, and gradually became darker in their recesses. Mont Blanc was before us, but it was covered with cloud; its base, furrowed with dreadful gaps, was seen above. **Pinnacles of** snow intolerably bright, part of the chain **connected** with Mont Blanc, shone through the clouds at intervals on high. I never knew, I never imagined, what mountains were before. The immensity of these aërial summits excited, when they suddenly burst upon the sight, a sentiment of ecstatic wonder, not unallied to madness: and remember, this was all one scene, it all pressed home to our regard and our imagination. Though it embraced a vast extent of space, the snowy pyramids which shot into the bright blue sky seemed to overhang our path; the ravine, clothed with gigantic pines and black with its depth below, so deep that the very roaring of the untameable Arve, which rolled through it, could not be heard above, all was as much our own as if we had been the creators of such impressions in the minds of others as now occupied our own. Nature was the poet, whose harmony held our spirits more breathless than that of the divinest.

As we entered the Valley of Chamouni, (which in fact may be considered as a continuation of those which we have followed from Bonneville and Cluses,) clouds hung upon the mountains at the distance perhaps of 6000 feet from the earth, but so as effectually to conceal not only Mont Blanc, but the other Aiguilles, as they call them here, attached and subordinate to it. We were travelling along the valley, when suddenly we heard a sound as of the burst of smothered thunder rolling above; yet there was something earthly in the sound, that told us it could not be thunder. Our guide hastily pointed out to us a part of the mountain opposite, from whence the sound came. It was an avalanche. We saw the smoke of its path among the rocks, and continued to hear at intervals the bursting of its fall. It fell on the bed of a torrent, which it displaced, and presently we saw its tawny-coloured waters also spread themselves over the ravine which was their couch.

We did not, as we intended, visit the Glacier des Bossons to-day, although it descends within a few minutes' walk of the road, wishing to survey it at least when unfatigued. We saw this glacier, which comes close to the fertile plain, as we passed: its surface was broken into a thousand unaccountable figures: conical and pyramidical crystallisations, more than fifty feet in height, rise from its surface, and precipices of ice of dazzling splendour overhang the woods and meadows of the vale. This glacier winds upwards from the valley, until it joins the masses of frost from which it was produced above, winding through its own ravine like a bright belt flung over the black region of pines. There is more in all these scenes than mere magnitude of proportion: there is a majesty of outline: there is an awful grace in the very colours which invest these wonderful shapes, a charm which is peculiar to them, quite distinct even from the reality of their unutterable greatness.

July 24.

Yesterday morning we went to the source of the Arveiron. It is about a league from this village; the river rolls forth impetuously from an arch of ice, and spreads itself in many streams over a vast space of the valley, ravaged and laid bare by its inundations. The glacier by which its waters are nourished, overhangs this cavern and the plain, and the forests of pine which surround it, with terrible precipices of solid ice; on the other side rises the immense Glacier of Montanvert, fifty miles in extent, occupying a chasm among mountains of inconceivable height, and of forms so pointed and abrupt, that they seem to pierce the sky. From this glacier we saw, as we sat on a rock, close to one of the streams of the Arveiron, masses of ice detach themselves from on high and rush with a loud dull noise into the vale. The violence of their fall turned them into powder, which flowed over the rocks in imitation of waterfalls, whose ravines they usurped and filled.

In the evening I went with Ducrée, my guide, the only tolerable person I have seen in this country, to visit the Glacier des Bossons. This glacier, like that of Montanvert, comes close to the vale, overhanging the green meadows and the dark woods with the dazzling whiteness of its precipices and pinnacles, which are like spires of radiant crystal, covered with a network of frosted silver. These glaciers flow perpetually into the valley, ravaging in their slow but irresistible progress the pastures and the forests which surround them, performing a work of desolation in ages, which a river of lava might accomplish in an hour, but far more irretrievably; for where the ice has once descended, the hardiest plant refuses to grow; if even, as in some extraordinary instances, it should recede after its progress has once commenced. The glaciers perpetually move onward, at the rate of a foot each day, with a motion that commences at the spot where, on the boundaries of perpetual congelation, they are produced by the freezing of the waters which arise from the partial melting of the eternal snows. They drag with them from the regions whence they derive their origin, all the ruins of the mountain, enormous rocks, and immense accumulations of sand and stones. These are driven onwards by the irresistible stream of solid ice; and when they arrive at a declivity of the mountain sufficiently rapid, roll down scattering ruin. I saw one of these rocks which had descended in the spring, (winter here is the season of silence and safety,) which measured forty feet in every direction.

The verge of a glacier like that of Bossons presents the most vivid image of desolation that it is possible to conceive. No one dares to approach it; for the enormous pinnacles of ice which perpetually fall, are perpetually reproduced. The pines of the forest, which bound it at one extremity, are overthrown and shattered to a wide extent at its base. There is something inexpressibly dreadful in the aspect of the few branchless trunks, which nearest to the ice-rifts still stand in the uprooted soil. The meadows perish, overwhelmed with sand and stones. Within this last year, these glaciers have advanced three hundred feet into the valley. De Saussure, the naturalist, says that they have their periods of increase and decay: the people of the country hold an opinion entirely different; but as I judge, more probable. It is agreed by all, that the snow on the summit of Mont Blanc and the neighbouring mountains perpetually augments, and that ice in the form of glaciers subsists without melting in the Valley of Chamouni during its transient and variable summer. If the snow which produces this glacier must augment, and the heat of the valley is no obstacle to the perpetual existence of such masses of ice as have already descended into it, the consequence is obvious; the glaciers must augment and will subsist, at least until they have overflowed this vale.

I will not pursue Buffon's sublime but gloomy theory, that this globe which we inhabit will at some future period be changed into a mass of frost by the encroachments of the polar ice and of that produced on the most elevated points of the earth. Do you, who assert the supremacy of Ahriman, imagine him throned among these desolating snows, among these palaces of Death and Frost, so sculptured in this their terrible magnificence by the adamantine hand of Necessity, and that he casts around him, as the first essays of his final usurpation, avalanches, torrents, rocks, and thunders, and above all these deadly glaciers, at once the proof and symbols of his reign; add to this, the degradation of the human species, who in these regions are half deformed or idiotic, and most of whom are deprived of anything that can excite interest or admiration. This is a part of the subject more mournful and less sublime; but such as neither the poet nor the philosopher should disdain to regard.

This morning we departed, on the promise of a fine day, to visit the Glacier of Montanvert. In that part where it fills a slanting valley, it is called the Sea of Ice. This valley is 950 *toises*, or 7600 feet, above the level of the sea. We had not proceeded far before the rain began to fall, but we persisted

until we had accomplished more than half of our journey, when we returned wet through.

Chamouni, July 25.

We have returned from visiting the Glacier of Montanvert or, as it is called, the Sea of Ice, a scene in truth of dizzying wonder. The path that winds to it along the side of the mountain, now clothed with pines, now intersected with snowy hollows, is wide and steep. The Cabin of Montanvert is three leagues from Chamouni, half of which distance is performed on mules, not so sure-footed but that on the first day the one which I rode fell in what the guides call a *Mauvais Pas*, so that I narrowly escaped being precipitated down the mountain. We passed over a hollow covered with snow, down which vast stones are accustomed to roll. One had fallen the preceding day, a little time after we had returned: our guides desired us to pass quickly, for it is said that sometimes the least sound will accelerate their descent. We arrived at Montanvert, however, safe.

On all sides precipitous mountains, the abodes of unrelenting frost, surround this vale: their sides are banked up with ice and snow, broken, heaped high, and exhibiting terrific chasms. The summits are sharp and naked pinnacles, whose overhanging steepness will not even permit snow to rest upon them. Lines of dazzling ice occupy here and there their perpendicular rifts, and shine through the driving vapours with inexpressible brilliance: they pierce the clouds like things not belonging to this earth. The vale itself is filled with a mass of undulating ice, and has an ascent sufficiently gradual even to the remotest abysses of these horrible deserts. It is only half a league, (about two miles,) in breadth, and seems much less. It exhibits an appearance as if frost had suddenly bound up the waves and whirlpools of a mighty torrent. We walked some distance upon its surface. The waves are elevated about twelve or fifteen feet from the surface of the mass, which is intersected by long gaps of unfathomable depth, the ice of whose sides is more beautifully azure than the sky. In these regions everything changes, and is in motion. This vast mass of ice has one general progress, which ceases neither day nor night; it breaks and bursts for ever; some undulations sink while others rise; it is never the same. The echo of rocks, or of the ice and snow which fall from their overhanging precipices or roll from their aërial summits, scarcely ceases for one moment. One would think that Mont Blanc, like the God of the Stoics, was a vast animal, and that the frozen blood for ever circulated through his stony veins.

We dined, M., C., and I, on the grass in the open air, surrounded by this scene. The air is piercing and clear. We returned down the mountain, sometimes encompassed by the driving vapours, sometimes cheered by the sunbeams, and arrived at our inn by seven o'clock.

Montalègre, *July* 28.

The next morning we returned through the rain to St. Martin. The scenery had lost something of its immensity, thick clouds hanging over the highest mountains; but visitings of sunset intervened between the showers, and the blue sky shone between the accumulated clouds of snowy whiteness which brought them, the dazzling mountains sometimes glittered through a chasm of the clouds above our heads; and all the charm of its grandeur remained. We repassed Pont Pélissier, a wooden bridge over the Arve and the ravine of the Arve. We repassed the pine forests which overhang the defile, the Château of St. Michel, a haunted ruin, built on the edge of a precipice and shadowed over by the eternal forest. We repassed the Vale of Servoz, a vale more beautiful, because more luxuriant, than that of Chamouni. Mont Blanc forms one of the sides of this vale also, and the other is inclosed by an irregular amphitheatre of enormous mountains, one of which is in ruins, and fell fifty years ago into the higher part of the valley: the smoke of its fall was seen in Piedmont, and people went from Turin to investigate whether a volcano had not burst forth among the Alps. It continued falling many days, spreading, with the shock and thunder of its ruin, consternation into the neighbouring vales. In the evening we arrived at St. Martin. The next day we wound through the valley which I have described before, and arrived in the evening at our home.

We have bought some specimens of minerals and plants and two or three crystal seals at Mont Blanc, to preserve the remembrance of having approached it. There is a Cabinet of *Histoire Naturelle* at Chamouni, just as at Keswick, Matlock, and Clifton, the proprietor of which is the very vilest specimen of that vile species of quack, that together with the whole army of *Aubergistes* and guides, and indeed the entire mass of the population, subsist on the weakness and credulity of travellers as leeches subsist on the sick. The most interesting of my purchases is a large collection of all the seeds of rare Alpine plants, with their names written upon the outside of the papers that contain them. These I mean to colonise in my garden in England, and to permit you to make what choice you please from them. They are companions which the

Celandine, the classic Celandine, need not despise; they are as wild and more daring than he, and will tell him tales of things even as touching and sublime as the gaze of a vernal poet.

Did I tell you that there are troops of wolves among these mountains? In the winter they descend into the valleys, which the snow occupies six months of the year, and devour everything that they can find out of doors. A wolf is more powerful than the fiercest and strongest dog. There are no bears in these regions. We heard, when we were at Lucerne, that they were occasionally found in the forests which surround that lake. Adieu.

S.

MONT BLANC

LINES WRITTEN IN THE VALE OF CHAMOUNI

I

The everlasting universe of things
Flows through the mind, and rolls its rapid waves,
Now dark,—now glittering,—now reflecting gloom,—
Now lending splendour, where from secret springs
The source of human thought its tribute brings
Of waters,—with a sound but half its own,
Such as a feeble brook will oft assume
In the wild woods, among the mountains lone,
Where waterfalls around it leap for ever,
Where woods and winds contend, and a vast river
Over its rocks ceaselessly bursts and raves.

II

Thus thou,—Ravine of Arve,—dark deep ravine,—
Thou many-coloured, many-voicèd vale,
Over whose pines and crags and caverns sail

Fast cloud-shadows and sunbeams; awful scene,
Where Power in likeness of the Arve comes down
From the ice-gulfs that gird his secret throne,
Bursting through these dark mountains like the flame
Of lightning through the tempest;—thou dost lie,
Thy giant brood of pines around thee clinging,
Children of elder time, in whose devotion
The chainless winds still come and ever came
To drink their odours, and their mighty swinging
To hear, an old and solemn harmony;
Thine earthly rainbows stretched across the sweep
Of the ethereal waterfall, whose veil
Robes some unsculptured image; the strange sleep
Which, when the voices of the desert fail,
Wraps all in its own deep eternity;
Thy caverns echoing to the Arve's commotion,
A loud lone sound no other sound can tame;
Thou art pervaded with that ceaseless motion,
Thou art the path of that unresting sound,
Dizzy Ravine! And, when I gaze on thee,
I seem, as in a trance sublime and strange,
To muse on my own separate phantasy,
My own, my human Mind, which passively
Now renders and receives fast influencings,
Holding an unremitting interchange
With the clear Universe of Things around;

One legion of wild thoughts, whose wandering
    wings
Now float above thy darkness, and now rest
Where that or thou art no unbidden guest,
In the still cave of the witch Poesy,
Seeking, among the shadows that pass by,
Ghosts of all things that are some shade of thee,
Some phantom, some faint image ; till the breast
From which they fled recalls them, thou art there !

III

Some say that gleams of a remoter world
Visit the soul in sleep, that death is slumber,
And that its shapes the busy thoughts outnumber
Of those who wake and live. I look on high ;
Has some unknown Omnipotence unfurled
The veil of life and death ? or do I lie
In dream, and does the mightier world of sleep
Spread far around and inaccessibly
Its circles ? For the very spirit fails,
Driven like a homeless cloud from steep to steep
That vanishes among the viewless gales !
Far, far above, piercing the infinite sky,
Mont Blanc appears,—still, snowy, and serene.
Its subject mountains their unearthly forms
Pile round it, ice and rock ; broad vales between
Of frozen floods, unfathomable deeps,

Blue as the overhanging heaven, that spread
And wind among the accumulated steeps;
A desert peopled by the storms alone,
Save when the eagle brings some hunter's bone,
And the wolf tracks her there. How hideously
Its shapes are heaped around!—rude, bare, and high,
Ghastly and scarred and riven! Is this the scene
Where the old Earthquake-dæmon taught her young
Ruin? Were these their toys? or did a sea
Of fire envelope once this silent snow?
None can reply: all seems eternal now.
The wilderness has a mysterious tongue
Which teaches awful doubt,—or faith so mild,
So solemn, so serene, that Man may be,
But for such faith, with Nature reconciled;
Thou hast a voice, great Mountain, to repeal
Large codes of fraud and woe; not understood
By all, but which the wise and great and good
Interpret, or make felt, or deeply feel.

IV

The fields, the lakes, the forests, and the streams,
Ocean, and all the living things that dwell
Within the dædal earth, lightning, and rain,
Earthquake and fiery flood and hurricane,

The torpor of the year when feeble dreams
Visit the hidden buds, or dreamless sleep
Holds every future leaf and flower, the bound
With which from that detested trance they leap,
The works and ways of man, their death and birth,
And that of him, and all that his may be,
All things that move and breathe, with toil and sound
Are born and die, revolve, subside and swell.
Power dwells apart in its tranquillity
Remote, serene, and inaccessible:
And this, the naked countenance of earth,
On which I gaze, even with these primæval mountains
Teach the adverting mind. The glaciers creep,
Like snakes that watch their prey, from their far fountains,
Slow rolling on; there, many a precipice
Frost and the sun in scorn of mortal power
Have piled: dome, pyramid, and pinnacle,
A city of death, distinct with many a tower
And wall impregnable of beaming ice,
Yet not a city, but a flood of ruin
Is there, that from the boundaries of the sky
Rolls its perpetual stream; vast pines are strewing
Its destined path, or in the mangled soil

Branchless and shattered stand; the rocks, drawn
    down
From yon remotest waste, have overthrown
The limits of the dead and living world,
Never to be reclaimed. The dwelling-place
Of insects, beasts, and birds, becomes its spoil;
Their food and their retreat for ever gone,
So much of life and joy is lost. The race
Of man flies far in dread; his work and dwelling
Vanish, like smoke before the tempest's stream,
And their place is not known. Below, vast caves
Shine in the rushing torrents' restless gleam,
Which from those secret chasms in tumult welling
Meet in the vale ; and one majestic River,
The breath and blood of distant lands, for ever
Rolls its loud waters to the ocean-waves,
Breathes its swift vapours to the circling air.

v

Mont Blanc yet gleams on high : the power is there,
The still and solemn power, of many sights
And many sounds, and much of life and death.
In the calm darkness of the moonless nights,
In the lone glare of day, the snows descend
Upon that Mountain ; none beholds them there,
Nor when the flakes burn in the sinking sun,

Or the star-beams dart through them.   Winds
    contend
Silently there, and heap the snow, with breath
Rapid and strong, but silently.   Its home
The voiceless lightning in these solitudes
Keeps innocently, and like vapour broods
Over the snow.   The secret Strength of Things
Which governs thought, and to the infinite dome
Of heaven is as a law, inhabits thee ;
And what were thou and earth and stars and sea,
If to the human mind's imaginings,
Silence and solitude were vacancy ?

INDEX

Acroceraunia, 49
Ahriman, 100, 184
Aiguilles, 9, 86, 94-6, 99
Alps, 4, 12-13, 27-9, 34, 46, 65, 69, 70-1, 74, 82-3, 86, 112, 133-4, 155-61, 174, 188
Ancœur, 20
Argos, 55
Arve, 9-11, 59, 69-72, 77, 85-6, 159, 174-9, 186, 190-1, 195
Arveiron, 9, 10, 68, 92, 102, 181
Aube, 24, 126

Bala, Lake, 53
Balmat, Jacques, 91-2
Balme, 74-5
Bar-sur-Aube, 26, 126
Barce, 24
Basle, 38, 140
Bear, 83-4, 91
Bécassine, 55
Bellerive, 48
Berne, 52, 63, 162
Besançon, 28-30, 43, **127-9**
Besolet (tern), 55, 164
Bethgelert, 75-84, 178
Blair, Charles, 93-4
Blücher, 24-5, 62
Bonn, 39-41, 146
Bonnant, 71, 86
Bonneville, 69-73, **174, 179**
Bonnivard, 62-4
Bossons, Glacier des, 9, 68, 88-9, 102, 181-3, 194
Boulogne, 18, 114, 116
Bouquetin (ibex), 82-3, 99, 178
Bourmont, General, 21-2

Bourrit, M. Th., 75, 78-9, 83, 87-9, 93-4, 99, 105
Bouverie, Tour de la, 61, 168
Brunnen, 11, 36-7, 135-7
Buffon, 99, 184
Byron, Lord, 3-6, 14, 40, 46-66, 144, 161-9

Cæsar's Towers, 21, 43, 52, 161
Caillet, Fountain of, 92, 102
Calais, 17-8, 114-5
Carrier, 91
Celandine, 103, 189
Chablais, 34
Chamois, 82-3, 91, 99, 178
Chamouni, 1, 12, 50, 53, 68-9, 75, 80-1, 83-91, 94-8, 112, 174-89, 185-9
Champagnolles, 46, 153
Champlitte, 126
Chapuis, 48
Charenton, 19, 20, 119
Chaumont, 26, 126
Chède, 79, 80
Chêne, 69
Chillon, 14, 61-4, 112, 170
Chimari, 49
Clarens, 4-7, 57, 61, 64, 112, 169-71
Cleves, 42, 146-7
Cluses, 69-73, 81, 174-5, 179
Coligny, 48
Coliseum, 80
Cologne, 42, 144, 146
Contamines, 69
Coolidge, W. A. B., 89, 93-4, 105
Cossacks, 21-6, 121-6
Courmayeur, 99

INDEX

Couteran, 89, **94**
Couttet, 98
Coxe, W., **93**

DAUPHINÉ, 70, **102**
Deyverdun, 65
Dent du Midi, 70, **72**
Dent d'Oche, 56
Deschamps, Joseph, 80, **82**
Desportes, Félix, 94
Dettingen, **140**
Dijon, 45, 152
Diodati, 40, 48
Dôle, 45, 152
Donati, 71
Doubs, 28, 33
Dover, 17, 113
Drance, 55, 164
Ducrée, 88
Dumas, 53, 64, 91-2, 105

ECHEMINE, 23, 124
Eckermann, 29, 105
Eden, F. M., 74, 77, 90, 94, **106**
Ehrenbreitstein, 40
Evian, 56, 164-5

FAUCIGNY, **69,** 70, **81**
Ferra, 53
Fish, 52-3, 162
Florian, 92
Foully, 81, 84
Frankenstein, 37, 39, 47-8, 74-5, 85-7, 92, 95, 107

GENEVA, 34, **43, 50, 62,** 155-9
———, Lake of, 46, 50-67, 155, 161-73
Génipi (yarrow), **99**
Gex, 46, 154
Gibbon, 65-6, 106, 172
Glaciers, 9, 68, 87-7, **102, 180-3**
Glarus, 82
Godwin, W., 16
Goethe, 29, **37-8,** 93
Gray, 126
Gray, Thomas, 34, 53, **84, 106**
Greece, 49, 54, 163
Gria, 87-8
Grisons, 84
Grosbois, 120

Gruner, G. S., 97, 106
Guignes, 20-1, 120
Gwynniad, 53

HERMANCE, 52, 161-2
Horace, 16, 56
Hugo, Victor, **11,** 63, **106**

IBEX (Ibsch), 82-3, 99, **178**

JURA, 27, 33, 45, 48-9, **84,** 152, 157-8
Jurine, L., **81**

KOCH, F., 106

LA CONDAMINE, 27, 98, 106
Lambard, 91
Langres, 26-7, 81, **126**
La Rothière, 24-5
Lausanne, 65-7, 171-2
Lavallette, 45, 151
Leschevin, 72, 81, 93, 106
Les Rousses, 13, 46, 154-5
Loffenburg, 38, 139-40
Lucerne, 11, 35-8, 84, 134-8, **156,** 189

MAASLUYS, 44, 149
Macdonald, Marshal, 25
Magland, 75-6, 175
Mannheim, 39, 143
Marlow, 103
Marne, 26
Martigny, 91
Matlock, 74-5, 175, **188**
Mayence, 39, 141, 143
Medwin, T., 19, 40, 80, 106
Meillerie, 4-6, 52, 56-61, 67, 112, 166, 173, 175
Ménoge, 69
Mercure Suisse, 97, 106
Milton, 3, 6, 48
Mines, 81, 85, 102, 178
Mer de Glace, 60, 92-103, **181,** 184-5
Mont Argentière, **47**
    Blanc, 6-9, 27-9, 45-9, 65, 69, **70,** 74-7, 82-92, 100-2, 156-9, 172, 178-96
    Brezon, 70

INDEX

Mont Cenis, 27, 84
   Chatelard, 81
   Iséran, 82
   Mallet, 99
   Morche, 72
   Rosenberg, 71
   Salève, 50, 60, 69, 159, 174
   Varens, 78
   Vaudagne, 85
Montague, Lady Mary W., 42-4, 107, 147
Montalègre, 8, 48-51, 68, 102, 161, 173
Montagne Maudite, 70
Montanvert, 68, 89, 92-3, 102, 181-7
Montées, 84-5
Montreux (Clarens), 1, 3-7, 57, 61, 64, 112, 169-71
Moore, J., 53, 74, 95-6, 99, 107
Mormant, 20
Mort, 29, 128
Mumph, 140

Nant d'Arpenaz, 10, 11, 75-6, 175-6
   Nayin, 87
   Sauvage, 86
Nangy, 69
Napoleon, 15, 20-5, 45, 57, 118, 120, 123
Napoli di Romania, 55
Necker, J., 79
Nerni, 52, 162-4
Neuchâtel, 24, 28-35, 53, 125, 133, 138, 152
Nimeguen, 43-4, 147
Nion, 46, 154
Noë, 31, 129
Nogent, 21-2, 121

Ouches, 87
Ouchy, 51, 65, 171-3
Oudinot, Marshal, 26

Paccard, Dr., 91-2, 107
Paccard Museum, 90
Pahlen, Count de, 22
Paradis, Marie, 91
Paris, 15, 18-20, 45, 53, 116-8, 133, 138, 150-3

Passi, 78
Pavillon, 23, 124
Payot, D., 90, 102
Payot, P., 92
Peacock, T. L., 50, 68, 84, 100, 161, 173, 184
Piedmont, 161, 188
Pilatus, 11, 12
Plainpalais, 48, 50, 159
Plantin, J. B., 82, 107
Platow, Hetman, 21
Pliny, 47, 68
Pococke, R., 78, 93, 97
Poligny, 45-6, 152
Pontarlier, 31-2, 45, 130-1
Pontecoulant, L. D., 94
Pont Pélissier, 7, 9, 77, 85-6, 187
Praz d'Avaz, 102
Prieuré, 89
Provins, 20, 76, 120-1
Pyrenees, 20, 76

Quixote, 19, 20, 48, 120

Ray, J., 18, 60, 82-3
Reposoir, 73
Reuss, 38, 138-9
Rheinfelden, 39, 40
Rhine, 1, 4, 13, 14, 38-41, 56, 103, 112, 138-9, 144-6, 149, 165
Rhone, 53, 59, 61, 159, 168-71
Rossetti, W. M., 9
Rotterdam, 41-2, 44, 149
Rousseau, 16, 34, 50-2, 57, 64-5
Rouai, 25

St. Aubin, 22, 121
St. Bernard, 57, 69, 70
St. Denis, 18, 117
St. Gervais, 77, 79, 86
St. Gingoux, 57, 59-61, 167-9
St. Gothard, 36, 103, 134
St. Julien, 168-9
St. Martin, 76-7, 88-9, 176-7, 187-8
St. Quiriace, 21
St. Sulpice, 33, 132
St. Victor, 62
St. Michel, Château, 85, 187
Ste. Germaine, 26
Sallanches, 69, 77-8, 89, 176
Salzburg, 83

INDEX

Sardinia, 34, 71, 161
Saussure, De, 70, 89-93, 96, 98, 107, 183
Savoy, 34, 61-3, 65, 69, 73, 82, 96, 164, 169
Schiller, 35
Schwytz, 36
Sècheron, 13, 46, 151, 155-6
Seine, 19, 23-4, 53, 119
Servoz, 71, 74, 77-8, 80-6, 177-8, 187
Shakespeare, 3, 4
Shelley, M., 16-20, 24, 31, 42-3, 69, 107-8. (*See* Frankenstein)
Shelley, P. B.
  First tour, 1-44, 111-50
  Early Poems, 6-14, 30-1, 36, 49, 60, 67, 70, 101, 190
  Journey to Geneva, 45-50, 151-61
  A Sail round the Lake, 51-67, 161-73
  Journey to Chamouni, 68-88, 173-9
  Glaciers of Chamouni, 88-103, 179-89
  References to Milton, 3, 6, 48
  To Shakespeare, 3, 5
  To Wordsworth, 2-6, 103-4, 189
Soleure, 35
Spezia, 58
Stolzenfels, 40
Strasburg, 39, 142

Tacitus, 16, 38, 47, 137
Taconnay, 87-8
Tairraz, 87, 91
Talèfre, 99, 103

Tell, 38, 136
Teneriffe, 27
Tennyson, 76
Tiel, 147
Tournier, 91
Trelawny, E. J., 58, 108
Trelliard, General, 20-1
Tripolitza, 55
Trois-Maisons, 122
Troyes, 20-5, 28, 45, 121, 124-5, 128, 130, 152
Turin, 70, 188
Tyrol, 82

Ulleswater, 53
Uri, 36-7, 134-6

Valais, 61, 65, 83-4, 95, 103, 168-9, 171
Valmy, Comte de, 20-1
Val Travers, 35
Vandœuvres, 25-6, 125
Vaud, Pays de, 47, 61, 172
Verviers, 33
Vevey, 50, 53, 64-7, 112, 161, 169, 171
Villeneuve, 61
Voirol, Col, 22

Walpole, H., 53, 84
White Mountain, 27
Windham, 93
Wolf, 84, 189
Wollstonecraft, M., 16, 39, 108, 141
Wordsworth, 2-6, 18, 41, 103, 108, 189

Yvron, 20

Printed by BALLANTYNE, HANSON & Co.
London & Edinburgh

www.ingramcontent.com/pod-product-compliance
Lightning Source LLC
Chambersburg PA
CBHW031740230426
43669CB00007B/425